SECURING BARITONE, BASS-BARITONE, AND BASS VOICES

Securing Baritone, Bass-Baritone, and Bass Voices

Richard Miller

OXFORD
UNIVERSITY PRESS

2008

OXFORD
UNIVERSITY PRESS

Oxford University Press, Inc., publishes works that further
Oxford University's objective of excellence
in research, scholarship, and education.

Oxford   New York
Auckland   Cape Town   Dar es Salaam   Hong Kong   Karachi
Kuala Lumpur   Madrid   Melbourne   Mexico City   Nairobi
New Delhi   Shanghai   Taipei   Toronto

With offices in
Argentina   Austria   Brazil   Chile   Czech Republic   France   Greece
Guatemala   Hungary   Italy   Japan   Poland   Portugal   Singapore
South Korea   Switzerland   Thailand   Turkey   Ukraine   Vietnam

Published by Oxford University Press, Inc.
198 Madison Avenue, New York, New York 10016

www.oup.com

Oxford is a registered trademark of Oxford University Press

Library of Congress Cataloging-in-Publication Data
Miller, Richard, 1926–
Securing baritone, bass-baritone, and bass voices / Richard Miller.
   p.   cm.
Includes bibliographical references and index.
ISBN 978-0-19-532265-1
1. Singing—Instruction and study. 2. Baritone (Singers)—Training of.
3. Bass-baritones—Training of. 4. Basses (Singers)—Training of.   I. Title.
MT820.M5992 2007
   782.8'814—dc22   2006051353

9   8   7   6   5   4   3   2   1

Printed in the United States of America
on acid-free paper

Honoring the Memorable Artistry of Leonard Warren

PREFACE

This book comes in response to colleagues, singers, and readers of books I have previously written who have asked for additional details on specific problems encountered by baritones, bass-baritones, and basses at all stages of development. Much of the book is directed to the practical examination of recurring technical and performance questions, in language as direct as possible.

In anticipating a varied readership, I at first considered dividing the book into three sections: "The Young Low-Voiced Male," "The Emerging Professional Low Voice," and "The Established Professional Low Voice." I discarded that plan because maneuvers for securing a well-produced sound can never be cast aside at any level of development or maturity. It matters not if the singer is early in his vocal journey or if he is an established artist; he must maintain unfailing vigilance of fundamental concepts. The road to attaining and preserving an elite singing voice is dependent on the constant renewal and revitalization of discernible principles that are put to use in daily praxis. In building a voice, specific areas of voice technique must at times be isolated and dealt with separately. But it is the daily specific regimen that renews and brings them together.

It is my hope that the reader will discover a progressive guideline for development, and that the topics considered will be read consecutively, so that the total sweep of systematic technique may become apparent. However, each chapter forms a more-or-less complete essay. It is my assumption that the advanced reader may have concern for explicit problems frequently experienced by low-voiced males, and may wish to begin directly with them. Several of the topics introduced in early chapters are later more fully explored at points along the technical continuum. As a result, rather frequent cross-referencing happens. Because the discipline of singing is an amalgamation of separate functions, it is inevitable that there will be some duplication of the technical areas as each particular technical problem is considered. Although the principles of vocalism are universal, each of the male low-voice categories has specific characteristics to be considered.

Some successful professional performers (even those who have acquired impressive performance credentials) encounter continuing difficulties from unresolved technical problems or from failure to remain faithful to a technical regimen. A wise singer incorporates all that he has earlier learned into his ongoing, consolidating process. This book proposes practical ways to help bring about such consolidation.

Any premise as to how great singing is acquired is meaningless unless it is directly applicable to performance of the standard literature. Vocal exercises have value only as they make possible the conquering of what the singer encounters in songs and arias. It is the plan of this manual to move directly from technical exercises to vocal literature excerpts. Some of the literature items I have chosen are appropriate to the less-advanced singer. Others lie clearly in the domain of the technically secure, mature singer. The instructor should assist the younger singer to select suitable items. Examples from which the more advanced singer may choose are identified.

It is a mistake to assume that fatiguing or driving the voice can build stamina. If any of the suggested examples from the literature cause a singer to experience vocal weariness those items should be discarded immediately until further development makes them appropriate. Nor should more than a few of the heavy literature segments (especially those in *verismo* style) be included within any single rehearsal period.

No one can claim to have answers to all the uncertainties an individual artist may encounter during a varied singing career. Yet frequently, one-sided techniques that advocate actions that are not locally controllable are put forward as solutions for every technical problem. The one-answer-teaching systems are inadequate because of what they do *not* cover. Among them are such concepts as: (1) every problem is simply a matter of correct "support" achieved by increasing tensions in the lower abdominal wall (the thoraco-abdominal mechanism) or, conversely, by inducing inward diaphragmatic fixation; (2) every technical deficiency can be alleviated through "tone placement" induced in all singers through identical subjective imagery; (3) conscious elevation of the soft palate—or conversely, palatal lowering; (4) the mandible (jaw) must be held in a constantly dropped position throughout vowel definition and all ranges of the voice, only the tongue moving for articulation; (5) the pharynx (throat) can be adjusted favorably by conscious pharyngeal spreading, with an unaltered throat position throughout the scale; (6) the chin and larynx must be elevated in order to free the voice; (7) laryngeal depression is essential to the production of a complete timbre; (8) laryngeal elevation is essential to the production of a complete timbre; (9) register separation strengthens the laryngeal musculature; (10) learning the names of muscles and organs, identifying the location of formants, the manner by which they are amplified, and knowing how to read spectrum analysis teaches one how to sing; and (11) forget about it all and just do what comes naturally while staying relaxed at all times!

Depending on what the need may be, one or more of the above "one-answer-fits-all" solutions may momentarily prove helpful. Even in the case of suggestions of intrinsic merit, none by itself represents an integrated system for dealing with the completeness of the vocal instrument.

Every baritone, bass-baritone, and bass should be wary of the teacher who does not apply the technical work of the studio to the performance literature but instead deals only with "voice functions." To say, "Songs and arias are the business of your coach, not your voice teacher," is to abdicate the better part of the singing teacher's responsibility. The purpose of vocal training is not to create singing machines capable of performing abstract vocalises or functions, but to create artists who can freely communicate text, drama, and music to a listening public.

I have given considerable care to assembling the select bibliography. It may appear daunting, but it contains the essence of voice pedagogy. If we are going to honestly ply the trade, we must be familiar with the tools of the trade as they have been defined by numerous authors over the centuries. Entries present a cross-section survey of historic and current pedagogic thought. Inclusions extend from celebrated treatises to a few imaginative, idiosyncratic speculations. Many aim to expand the bridge between subjective imagery and what is physiologically and acoustically knowable. A number of citations are from the voice-science field of the twentieth- and twenty-first centuries.

Great strides in helping the singer know what really works, and why it does, were made in the last half of the twentieth century and continue today. Through specific information, the aware singer avoids trial and error and time-consuming experimentation. By separating out the pedagogical wheat from the uncertain chaff, a reader will strengthen his or her critical judgment. The reader is urged, over a period of time, to sample as much of the reading material included in the select bibliography as possible.

Because I have witnessed many singers who struggle to put into practice maneuvers that cannot be carried out either physiologically or acoustically, I have devoted segments of this book to functional information. By no means do I believe that great singing can be produced simply by understanding how voice mechanics work. But I am convinced that if a singer tries to ingrain routines that go contrary to natural structure, his chances of achieving security are extremely reduced. If his automobile doesn't run properly, he doesn't need to be a mechanic to take care of it, but he does need to check with someone who knows how to correct the problem. An intelligent consumer carefully examines medication claims against what he knows about health, and seeks out qualified physicians. Accuracy of legal and financial advice is carefully investigated. Anyone who makes a serious investment in a performance career would be wise to examine the veracity of the principles by which he is being instructed.

It is highly probable that the user of this manual already has experienced conflicting pedagogical notions. It may well be that he has been through several conflicting systems without having found adequate answers to his questions. I invite him to weigh carefully what constitutes the factual and what constitutes the speculatively eccentric. The book aims to offer practical assistance in helping the singer in his personal search for secure technique.

Each individual professionally oriented voice, if handled efficiently, will itself ultimately divulge technical pathways to follow. The singing mentor's task is to help in removing impeding obstacles. Any change a singer is asked to make must feel better, sound better, and look better. It may at first feel, sound, and look different, but it should not hurt. It also ought to be aesthetically more pleasing in sensation, auditory response, and appearance than was previously the case.

Each singer follows a distinctive learning continuum. No singer is ready to initiate at the same time every technical skill considered in this book. A knowledgeable teacher, and the performer himself, will keep constantly in mind at what point on the developmental scale the singer has arrived, and will adapt accordingly. A singer should be wary of the new teacher who accepts a promising singer into his or her studio, and then says, "Now we have to start all over." Not all singers are at the same location on the developmental continuum, but each individual already has something of value or the teacher would not have accepted him into the studio in the first place. New information ought to be added to that which already works well.

Freedom in singing comes through coordinating natural processes, but it is not achieved by simply "doing what comes naturally." Free singing is made up of learned synchronization of maneuvers that most often must be separately mastered, then united into a concerted technical whole. Swimming may be a natural thing, but it has to be taught and learned. So in many respects with the voice of singing.

The key to freedom and efficiency of production is the recognition that each baritone, bass-baritone, or bass singer ought to function within the confines of his unique instrument. Singers should be cautious of joining a studio where "the studio sound" is imposed on every voice. Each voice has its own distinguishing characteristics. General technical principles are valid for all voices, but each singer must realize his own tonal ideal.

Not every singer of serious intent will have found a voice mentor with whom to work in concentrated fashion. Although many readers of this book probably have found a studio home, it is my hope that an advanced and established singer may independently discover areas of advice that will serve him in his personal search. Some of the topics presented will be pertinent to one singer but less to another. My aim is to assist in *securing* artistic and healthy vocalism for the active performer, and to assist the aspiring singer to move in that direction.

ACKNOWLEDGMENTS

Primary thanks are due to Oxford University Press's Kim Robinson for her encouragement in writing this book, and for her patience in awaiting its completion. Baritones Ferris Allen and Michael Weyandt deserve special recognition for assistance in the compilation of exercises and musical examples, and soprano Ami Vice has helped with manuscript preparation. I am deeply indebted to Mary, my wife, who smooths the way for all my endeavors, including this one. To the numerous voice researchers and the talented lower male voices with whom it has been my privilege to collaborate over half a century, and who have taught me much, I extend lasting gratitude.

CONTENTS

Part I

Technique

Chapter 1

WHO IS A BARITONE? WHO A BASS-BARITONE? WHO A BASS?

Voice category is largely determined by the dimensions of the larynx, the construction of the vocal tract, the structure of the respiratory and resonance systems (comprising the nostrils, the nasal cavities, the pharyngeal cavities, the oral cavity, the larynx, the trachea, the bronchi), and by overall body build. Most males are baritones. Tenors and basses are deviations from the norm.

Baritones may feel relieved to learn that they are not departures from the standard, but their satisfaction may be short-lived when they recognize that performance competition is greater within the baritone fach than in any other male category. The average male is a potential baritone.

In addition to the general SATB (soprano, alto, tenor, bass) designations, every major voice category has its subdivisions. Shades of demarcation among baritones are based on what may at first blush seem to be minimal physical and psychological variants. Lack of recognition of subtle attributes may lead to the establishment of false subcategory designations.

Every voice shares in a commonality of technical application, but each singer is unique and must be encouraged to respond in an individual way to specific instruction. Although universal techniques apply to all elite singing voices, the distinctiveness of each instrument must be primary. The final determinant will be the individual's singular concept of what constitutes beautiful timbre in his own voice.

The term baritone did not come into widespread usage until the first quarter of the nineteenth century. Before that, regardless of range or dramatic stipulations, opera and oratorio roles for low-voiced males were listed as the property of the bass singer. A number of roles composed in the late seventeenth and eighteenth centuries, and those by Handel and by Mozart and his contemporaries, were originally indicated for bass voice but are eminently suitable to the baritone or the bass-baritone.

With the growing demand for dramatic contrast among all types of voices, male singers became identified by subcategories: (1) baritone, (2) bass-baritone, and (3) bass. Certainly, roles in the operas of Mozart and Rossini forever altered the notion that male voices are either patently tenor or distinctly bass. Voices within these subcategories may be lyric or dramatic, calling forth additional labels such as lyric baritone, dramatic baritone, basso-cantante, lyric bass, and dramatic bass. In addition, there are "buffo" subdivisions to correspond to each of the "serious" categories.

Up to a point, voice categorization may match external physical appearance. A number of low-voiced males have long necks and prominent larynges. In the larynges of low-voiced males, there frequently is a visible external demarcation between the thyroid and the cricoid cartilages. With many low-voiced males, the entire laryngeal structure is larger, longer, and externally more defined than are those of high-voiced males. Most tenors are short-necked individuals who do not display large laryngeal prominences.

There is, however, great physical variation within wide-ranging male low-voiced structures. A number of baritones are also short-necked with larynges scarcely more externally visible than those of most tenors. Parenthetically, there are also physical aberrations among high-voiced males. Although teachers of singing commonly remark on generalities regarding physical appearance among persons of the same fach, and speculate as to how outward manifestation suggests voice category, external appearance is not a reliable indicator.

How to Determine a Male Voice Category

The scope of the speech-inflection range—to include the complete gamut of heightened spoken expression—is a strong determinant in revealing a male singer's voice category. Speech inflection is even more crucial in recognizing the male singing fach than it is for that of the female voice. Voice category is not based merely on how high or how low the singer can comfortably negotiate a scale. In both genders, the overriding consideration is the general character of tonal quality. How the singer handles the tessitura of the standard literature is another important determinant. As indicated earlier, much depends on the structure of the larynx and on the behavioral habits of the vocal folds (vocal cords).

Before examining traditional customs in category determination and in the practical application of resonance and registration practices essential to the low-voiced male, the singer will save future time and confusion about

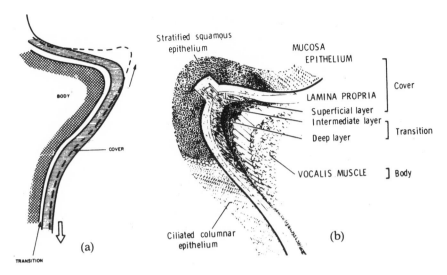

Figure 1.1. Vocal fold function (after Hirano and Stevens, *Vocal Fold Physiology*, 1981, Tokyo University Press)

what he may be told if he understands what is taking place physiologically in the voice qualities historically designated as "chest," "mixed," and "head" voice.

The paired vocal folds are a tripartite mechanism that consists of (1) a cover, (2) a transition material, and (3) a body made up of the vocalis muscle (see fig. 1.1).

In ascending pitch, the vocal folds elongate, an action that diminishes the mass of the folds, thereby increasing their elasticity. The singer perceives these events as the changing sensations of resonance. Lower pitches seem located in the chest, higher pitches in the head, and intermediate pitches between.

Janwillem van den Berg (1968, pp. 22–23) provides a precise description of the physical causes of voice registers, first pointing out the events of "chest voice." "Variations in this register [chest] are primarily brought about by variations in the internal tensions in the body of the vocal folds, i.e., by the contracting tensions in the vocalis muscle."

With regard to middle and upper registers, van den Berg explains that in middle voice (mixed voice or *zona di passaggio*) "the longitudinal forces in the vocal ligaments are no longer negligible compared with those in the vocalis muscle, but are of the same order of magnitude." As pitch ascends, contraction by the vocalis muscles (the thickest portion of the thyroarytenoid complex that includes the vocal folds) lessens. The ligaments of the vocal folds are stretched. As the scale ascends, there is a gradual process of change within the muscular complex, so that the vocal folds follow a different progression than that which occurs for pitches in low register.

The vocalis muscle controls the internal tensions in the body of the vocal folds and is a determinant of modal voice (so-called chest). When the vocal ligaments (intrinsic edges of the folds) are stretched, they elongate up to the point where they cannot further yield. This "chest" register is sometimes referred to as the "heavy mechanism," a pedagogic term popularized by William Vennard (who pursued important research with van den Berg).

Van den Berg's explanation clarifies laryngeal action in middle voice. He concludes (1968, 132–234):

> When the subject sings an ascending or a descending scale with no appreciable transition in sound quality, he needs to change gradually from one type of adjustment to the other. That means that the antagonistic active tensions in the vocalis muscles and the passive tensions in the vocal ligaments, together with the adduction of the glottis and the value of the flow of air, need to balance smoothly and gradually.

How is this complex function translated into the evenly registered male voice? Various voice pedagogies have proposed systems, often based on physiologically untenable assumptions. There are techniques that attempt to separate the registers, later to rejoin them. Registration-separation advocates carry so-called chest voice (modal register) into the upper regions of the voice. They ignore the balance of active tensions in the vocalis muscles, and the passive tensions in the vocal ligaments. They fail to take into account the cycle-per-second approximation of the vocal folds and the response of the folds to airflow, described so succinctly by van den Berg.

There are pedagogies that attempt to build the entire male upper range on the quality of falsetto (the imitative sound of the female voice in the male instrument). Falsetto, as understood in historic vocal pedagogy, does not equate with the upper-range timbre of the professional male voice. Stroboscopic examination undertaken at the Otto B. Schoepfle Vocal Arts Center (OBSVAC) at Oberlin Conservatory shows that vocal-fold approximation is generally less complete in male falsetto production than in balanced high-voice activity. (See chapter 10.)

Other teachers have sought to carry the "call of the voice" beyond regions of healthy function, with dependence on vocalis muscle inflexibility. In counterdistinction, the "just do it naturally" doctrine leads to a lack of energization essential to elite singing. International historic pedagogy avoids these pitfalls. What follows in these pages is based on historical premises, modern voice research, and on the performance history of finely tuned instruments of great past and contemporary singing artists.

Voice science (sometimes currently termed vocology) registration terminology refers to low pitches of the voice as "modal," the higher pitches as "falsetto." For the voice scientist, the middle range of the voice is usually described as a gradual adjustment of modal and falsetto registers. Traditional voice pedagogy refers to this intermediate range of middle voice as *voce media*, or the *zona di passaggio*. The term falsetto is reserved to describe the imitation of the female voice by the male, and the reinforced falsetto sound of the contemporary operatic countertenor.

In any consideration of voice registers, it must be mentioned in passing that research attention in recent decades has been drawn to a sound designated as a separate register: vocal fry. Fry resembles a prolonged vocal-fold rattle, a "frying" sound. Other terms to describe the sound are "glottal scrape," "click," or "creaky voice." Although vocal fry may serve in determining formant locations in voice research, it has no practical application for public performance. To attempt to build a technique on "vocal fry" is to depart from historic vocalism. There is no evidence, as is sometimes claimed, that fry improves both high or low registers. Fry has the character of a prolonged vocal noise. It suspiciously resembles the extended faulty onset of an unskilled singer.

As indicated earlier, the male tends to speak and inflect his voice far more extensively in modal register (the long male lower range) than does the female, producing a standard vocal timbre that most pedagogies term "chest." In actuality, the chest, filled as it is with spongy material called the lungs, is not an effective resonance contributor. However, through sympathetic vibration conveyed by bone conduction, for much of the male range the spoken and sung "chest" voices feel as though the chest were the primary vibrator. As will be explored later in this book, the singer or his teacher may unfortunately confuse the sensation of the sound with the source of the sound.

The female speaks mostly in so-called head, while the male depends on "chest" for speech. For example, at a moderate dynamic level, were the typical lyric baritone to inflect his speaking voice to its highest comfortable range, as in an indignant "*Well?*" or a firm "*Hello!*" he would seldom phonate beyond the pitch of B_3 (the pitch just below middle C [C_4]). That is, he would rarely inflect his normal speaking voice beyond the upper demarcation point of what is commonly termed his "chest register." Were he to raise the pitch and the energy level, or resort to shouting, he could manage a number of additional pitches (roughly another fourth) above that point. He would also fatigue his voice, were he to do so for an extended period.

Before discussing the pitch designations at which register events occur, we briefly digress to indicate pitch designations in the currently most widely used notation system. In each keyboard octave, beginning with the note C, a characteristic number is given that octave; for example, middle C is identified as C_4, the start of the fourth keyboard octave. Two octaves above, C_6 corresponds to high C. (Music for the low-voiced singer written in the treble clef is an octave lower than is the same pitch indication when sung by the female. Thus, high A for the baritone is actually A_4.)

The lower the pivotal point in the ascending scale at which speech inflection terminates, the lower the singing voice. This registration episode is known in historic international voice pedagogy as the *primo passaggio* (the first passage). In summary, the lyric baritone will most frequently experience his first register occurrence at B_3. For the more dramatic baritone, it will happen around Bb_3. For the bass-baritone, it occurs lower, generally at A_3. A basso may experience a similar event at Ab_3. A true *basso profondo* undergoes the same type of pivotal registration point at about G_3. (The lyric tenor will reach his first pivotal registration point at approximately D_4, the leggiero at Eb_4. The spinto tenor often displays the primo passaggio at $C\sharp_4$. The Heldentenor mostly experiences a similar phenomenon at C_4.)

The bass-baritone has an instrument whose registration events lie midway between those of baritone and bass categories. As suggested earlier, his easy speech-inflection range tends to terminate at about A_3. A singer who experiences this registration occurrence will most probably be a dramatic bass-baritone or a lyric bass. The singer whose unforced speech-inflection range concludes around G_3 is definitely a bass. In rare cases with the basso profondo, this register event will occur as low in the scale as $F\sharp_3$, resulting in the true *schwarzer* (black) bass.

Registration pivotal points can naturally occur at pitches that lie "in the cracks" between fixed keyboard hertz (Hz) pitches. The human voice is a glissando instrument. The vocal instrument is not geared to the lower pitch levels common to regional European cultural centers of past centuries, despite recent premises that postulate a natural relationship between the singing instrument and lower pitch systems. (There may be good reason to approve the campaign to lower the pitch A_4 from 440Hz to 420Hz, but it is not based on laryngeal structure, a configuration that varies from one voice category to the next.)

Roughly at the interval of a fourth above the first pivotal point in the scale lies the *secondo passaggio*. Between these two male-voice *passaggi* lodges a register negotiable by calling or shouting (as mentioned earlier), actions that are inappropriate to well-registered singing. For the male to shout beyond the secondo-passaggio pivotal point could prove painful and injurious, yet the trained singer learns to sing in that range by achieving resonance balances not normally present in the "call" range of the speaking voice.

The area between the two pivotal registration points—roughly the interval of a fourth—is designated as the *zona di passaggio* (the passage zone) or *voce media* (middle voice) (see chapter 6). The singer must learn to bridge areas of lower and upper ranges by means of vowel modification, accomplished by resonance balancing, and by an adjustment in breath-management levels. Much of what follows will be directed to those procedures.

Shortly after having undergone puberty, a youthful singer who has not had previous voice training will probably raise his larynx as he reaches the

TABLE I.   Zona di passaggio (pivotal registration points)

Category	Primo passaggio	Secondo passaggio
Lyric baritone	B_3	E_4
Dramatic (Verdi) baritone	Bb_3	Eb_4
Bass-baritone	A_3	D_4
Lyric bass	Ab_3	Db_4
Basso profondo	G_3	C_4

primo passaggio. The choral conductor of adolescent male voices may find assistance in discovering voice categorization by requesting a youth to sing a nine-note scale, beginning in low voice in a light "unsupported" timbre. The point at which the youngster is disposed to elevate his head (and therefore his larynx) generally occurs at the primo passaggio.

The problem of elevation of the head and larynx at the primo passaggio pivotal registration juncture is not reserved to the young singer. Even mature singers may resort to negotiating the upper range by having recourse to laryngeal elevation. Elevating the chin (which raises the larynx) in the passage zone continues to plague many adult male voices. Raising the larynx shortens the vocal tract and reduces the participation of lower harmonics. The result is a thinner quality of sound that stands as a barrier to a balanced scale. As has been seen, the category of male voice is determined by the location of the passaggi phenomena. Despite predictable patterns among male low voices, individual variations in the location of the passage zone exist. But, in general, pivotal registration locations within the male low voices can be charted as in table I.

The Lyric Baritone

Most of the opera and artsong literatures are written for the lyric baritone. The lyric baritone is destined to sing the major roles in the lyric theater. Many of opera's greatest baritone vehicles belong to him. Roles in operas by Rossini, Bellini, and Donizetti, a great deal of the French operatic literature, and the vast reservoir of the lied and the mélodie literature are his staples. The bel canto poles of agility and sostenuto are united in his literature. The lyric baritone serves as the backbone of the opera theater.

The Verdi Baritone

In today's opera world, the most coveted low-voice male instrument is the Verdi baritone. Verdi expanded expectations of the elite baritone voice. The Verdi baritone must have a powerful, rangy instrument. It must have size and power that competes with full orchestral sound, authority in complex ensembles and duets, the ability to present a low range that is capable of "projection," the ability to keep up a sustained voce media tessitura, and an upper range capable of brilliance and power. The category includes not only the operas of Verdi but of most of the composers who came after him. It includes a large portion of the baritone roles of the late-nineteenth-century Italian and French opera repertoires. The baritone *verismo* school of singing, so fully exploited by composers of the late nineteenth and twentieth centuries, became the heart of the operatic literature for the low-voiced male. It is the property of the Verdi baritone.

The Nonoperatic Baritone

The range extension and the sustained tessitura called for in much of the lied and the *mélodie* literatures of the nineteenth and twentieth centuries are best served through vocal lyricism. Characteristically, a substantial part of that repertoire does not rely on the dramatic vocal power found in much of the operatic literature. The timbres of many beautifully produced instruments are not well suited for opera roles. Operatic singing is not for everyone, a lesson not always learned by singers and their teachers.

A number of singers do not find themselves psychologically attuned to the high intensity roles required by the dramatic situations so routine to the opera stage. Fortunately, much of the vast and wonderful song literature belongs to them. But in today's performance world, it is difficult to build a career solely as an artsong, lieder, or mélodie singer. Most modern recital artists are also successful opera singers (see chapter 17).

In a contemporary reversal of operatic casting practices, in the musical theater (musical comedy) of the latter half of the twentieth century, the role of hero and lover often falls to the baritone, not to the tenor. The current popular entertainment idioms, in which male singers aim to sound castrated or unsexed, or as emotional screamers, represent categories beyond my competency to evaluate. I will refrain from offering uninformed comment regarding them.

The Baritenor

The registration occurrences of yet another common category of young male voice must be mentioned: the classical singer whose passage zone lies between C_4 and F_4. This type of voice has been described, usually pejoratively, as a *baritenor*, because initially there may be difficulty in determining whether the singer should be trained as a tenor or a baritone. Such singers are sometimes termed "second tenors," or even "A-flat tenors."

The C_4–F_4 pivotal zona di passaggio of an individual singer may indicate several viable possibilities: (1) a light lyric baritone, (2) a *Spieltenor* (an actor/tenor), or (3) a *Heldentenor* (*tenore robusto*). These categories are defined by widely disparate physical characteristics, yet all tend to display similar registration locations. Parenthetically, the Spieltenor is a singer capable of a wide rage of song literature and opera roles. He is often assigned the better comprimario tenor roles and should not be confused with the buffo tenor. The Heldentenor is the most robust of tenor instruments.

A singer whose zona di passaggio lodges between C_4 and F_4 would be well advised to adhere to the lyric baritone literature during early training. He should not too soon attempt the higher-lying tenor repertoire that may later become appropriate.

Much of the standard song literature lodges comfortably for the medium-ranged voice—thus is ideal for the baritenor. When the baritenor's technical production becomes sufficiently stable, his instrument will reveal its true permanent category. Yet there is a danger that the baritenor may settle on the baritone category without having sufficiently explored other possibilities. Many a potential tenor has been falsely classified as a baritone simply because his upper voice remained unexplored.

Because registration events may vary drastically within male low-voiced categories, it is unwise to affix identical rules of vowel modification or "cover" for all of them. Devising vowel-migration charts—as several courageous pedagogues have done—that rigidly apply to all male low voices is nonproductive and detrimental to the individuality of the singing voice.

The Bass-Baritone

As indicated in table 1, register events for the bass-baritone occur between those of the baritone and the bass. The bass-baritone combines the lyricism of the baritone with the richness of the bass. His timbre may remind of the baritone, or it may take on characteristics of the bass. The graciousness of a smoothly delivered bass-baritone quality is ideal for the projection of respected authority and personal warmth. With the resonance balance of his instrument, the bass-baritone is well equipped to sculpture dramatic character portrayals of both serious and comic proportions.

The Bass

A number of contemporary performing artists are listed as adhering to both the bass-baritone and the bass categories. Among all low-voice categories of the singing voice, the true bass is the most rare. His sonorous depth of quality is impressive. Much of his literature demands the same degree of velocity as that required of higher, lighter voices. The spectrum of roles for the bass covers a wide range from respected elder to sensuous lover. In addition, the bass buffo literature represents a major facet of potential repertoire. And much of the oratorio literature for low voice is the property of the bass singer. When the schooled bass voice possesses the capability of depth and brilliance, it is difficult to envision a more gratifying male timbre.

Chapter 2

BEGINNING IN THE SPEECH-INFLECTION RANGE (THE ONSET)

Registration and acoustic events encountered in other registers will later be considered but, for the moment, deliberation is restricted to the range in which the speaking voice is normally inflected. Before concentrating on upper-range extension, the wise singer (with his teacher) will look for freedom of production in the range of the singing voice that most closely parallels speech. It should be kept in mind that "vowelization" and "vocalization" have a common etymological origin. A frequent axiom found in early treatises on singing advised that, when singing in the speech-inflection range, one ought to sing as one speaks ("*Si canta come si parla*"). This admonition pertains to both acoustics and physiology, but "singing like speaking" is limited to the speech-inflection range. (Beyond the speech range, physiologic and acoustic alterations are necessitated.) Although the singer must learn to use his voice in highly specialized ways, his singing voice is the same instrument as the one with which he speaks. The dictum "one sings as one speaks, when in the speech-inflection range" stands in contradiction to systems that claim the speaking voice must be altered and rebuilt for the strenuous tasks of singing. There is a theory of voice training that claims to recover the primitive aspects of voicing, predicated on the premise that before the emergence of speech—presumably in some vocal Atlantis—the singing voice was uninhibited. In that singular technique, primitive nonspeech sounds are promoted in the hope of recovering the origins of the singing voice. (I will refrain from describing the batteries of sounds recommended by adherents of this somewhat bizarre technique.) Such assumptions are contrary to what is known anthropologically about the development of speech in prehistoric periods of early human existence.

Those who believe that the "resonant singing voice" is attainable only by altering the normal speaking voice will find "*si canta come si parla*" an unacceptable doctrine. In what follows, instructional advice is based on the centuries-old international presumption that the natural functions of the speaking voice must be honed and adapted to the needs of the song and opera literatures.

Making the Transition from Speech to Song

Series of exercises can alert the singer to resonance balancing. Primary among them is the onset, *l'attacco del suono*, advocated in numerous treatises of past centuries. The manner in which tone is initiated tends to determine the degree of freedom that will be demonstrated throughout the duration of a phrase.

EXERCISE 2.1

In normal speech range, have the singer speak a series of dynamic "Ha-ha-ha-ha-Ha!" expressions, imitative of the connected syllabification of laughter. Immediately repeat the onsets with the singing voice, in staccato fashion, on a 5–4–3–2–1 musical pattern, in an easy speech range—without altering the production from speech to song. Take an imperceptible, quiet breath between the onsets.

Exercise 2.1

EXERCISE 2.2

Sustain a single syllable over the 5–4–3–2–1 pattern.

Exercise 2.2

Remaining in the comfortable speech range, execute the quick, vital major third interval on 1–3–1, on the lateral vowel /e/ (as in the word "chaos"), then on the vowel /ɑ/ (as in the exclamation "Ah!"). Proceed by half tones through the keys of C, D♭, D, and E♭. Include other vowels of the lateral (front) and rounded (back) series (see appendix 3). Insist on the presence of vibrancy (see chapter 11).

Exercise 2.3

EXERCISE 2.4

Keeping in mind the quality of energized speech, extend the process through a quickly executed 1–3–5–3–1 pattern, alternating front and back vowels.

Exercise 2.4

Next, add the sequence 1–3–5—5–3–1. Observe a fermata on the fifth; take a silent breath renewal following the release at the fermata, then again at the prime. Accomplish in a few neighboring keys.

Exercise 2.5

Each onset must have a precise beginning and an exact release. The singer needs to consciously avoid two pitfalls associated with the onset: (1) breathy phonation, and (2) pressed phonation. Aspirated "Ha" begins with the vocal folds less than fully occluded. Aspiration must be brief and scarcely audible. With the emergence of the phoneme /ɑ/, the breath expulsion that produced the aspirated /h/ of "Ha" should be totally eliminated.

A second pitfall concerns pressed phonation. After securing the aspirated onset, the singer should turn to the glottal onset, characterized by a clean stroke of the glottis. (It must never become the *coup de glotte*, which was described by Garcia as a slight cough.) The two types of onset, aspirated and glottal, should be alternated. In order to avoid either excessive aspiration or too firm a glottal closure, it may be helpful only to *imagine* the prefix /h/. Never should the singer feel that air is passing over the vocal folds. Admonitions to "start the flow of breath, then add tone to it" are destructive to healthy phonation. In distinction to the notion of prefacing a sung phonation with airflow, Giovanni Battista Lamperti, as well as many of his followers, suggested that one should "sing on the gesture of inhalation." An accompanying Lamperti rubric asked, "Why get out of the position of singing in order to breathe, or out of the position of breathing in order to sing?" Renewal of the breath must become as automatic in the singing voice as in nonphonatory quiet breathing, the difference being that it is taken more deeply and can be sustained over a longer period of time.

I have found a useful pedagogic rubric for breath retention to be "suspend the moment of inhalation (inspiration) before executing the onset, and remain with that sensation throughout the phrase." The breath is suspended, not held.

Chapter 3

MANAGING THE BREATH

We seldom engage in long bursts of speech. In everyday communication, most phrases are of brief duration—often five or six seconds in length. Yet, in singing, we sustain phrases for much longer periods. It is not unusual to encounter high-lying sung phrases of more than ten seconds' duration. Extended melismatic passages may reach at least fifteen seconds—one need think only of how often Mozart, Brahms, Verdi, Strauss, Duparc, and Barber pile up series of lengthy phrases. In short, the duration factor is more extensive in song than in speech.

Although it is true that when we sing we are using the same breath mechanism as when we speak, the breath-management process is prolonged for elite sung production. Both speaking and singing are subject to specific events of the breath cycle. These actions in singing constitute a rhythmic dance that unites atmospheric pressure and subglottic pressure in a marvelously reflexive ballet. This cyclical sequence consists of the gesture of inhalation, the phonation itself (during which breath is being exhaled), and the immediate and silent renewal of the breath. Of utmost value is the rubric: "*The release is the new breath*" (see chapter 2).

The Respiratory Cycle

In most geographic locations, atmospheric pressure measures approximately fifteen pounds per square inch. As we inhale, the volume of the lung expands; we arrive at a subglottic pressure lower than the atmospheric pressure that surrounds us. The internal pressure (below the glottis) rises as air in the lung is depleted by phonation or exhalation. Within a short period of time, subglottic pressure exceeds that of atmosphere pressure, at which point we experience the need to replenish our breath; the entire cycle begins anew. For most persons, this reflex sequence in quiet, normal breathing occupies roughly four to five seconds, divided somewhat unequally between inhalation and expiration. The singer must learn to elongate the phonatory portion of the cycle by reducing the rate of breath emission and by automatically adjusting resistance to the exiting breath. Only under these conditions can the singing of phrases of varying duration be mastered.

Breath Management Methods

Management of the breath occupies a major portion of most pedagogic systems, many in contradiction to each other. These disagreements are encapsulated in the questing singer's "Should I be 'an in-and-upper' or 'a down-and-outer' breather?" (For a fuller examination of comparative pedagogic premises about breath management, see *National Schools of Singing, Revised,* 1997.) The in-and-up school (abdominal fixation) aims to control breath exit by a continuous inward firming of the abdominal and epigastric regions. The down-and-out school (*Bauchaussenstütze*) argues that the diaphragm can best be retained in its lowest position by outward, downward pressures on the abdominal wall, a technique sometimes known as "belly breathing." Both philosophies are based on misconceptions regarding the mechanical aspects of breath management. To more fully understand the controversy on "breath support," a few brief considerations of the physiology of the breath mechanism are in order. (Further information on the mechanics of breathing for singing is included in the select bibliography.)

The Role of the Diaphragm

Much confusion comes from false assumptions regarding the role of the diaphragm itself. The diaphragm lacks significant proprioceptive responses; it cannot be locally controlled. Most of the actions assigned to it by subjective, inventive voice pedagogues are simply not within the diaphragm's capabilities. Positions of the diaphragm are in part determined by the maneuvers of surrounding musculatures. Pushing out, or pulling downward, on the abdominal wall cannot fixate the diaphragm. Nor can the diaphragm be firmed in one location by inward abdominal pressure or thrusting. During the exit of the breath, the diaphragm remains essentially electrically silent (verifiable by EMG [electromyographic] examination).

The diaphragm sits higher in the thorax than is generally envisioned by most teachers and singers. The central tendon of the diaphragm lodges at about the fifth rib—the level of the nipple. Attached to the heart and anchored posteriorly at the spine, the diaphragm does not go plunging downward for high notes and surging upward for low notes, as some would have it, nor does it engage in the reverse process. Much of its action is reflexive. "Control" of the diaphragm can be achieved only by the concerted action of the musculature surrounding the diaphragm and the abdomen (see fig. 3.1), through a learned regulation of the airflow. To tell the singer to sing "with" or "from" the diaphragm is illusory advice. Such admonitions can only refer to events that take place around and below the diaphragm itself. The diaphragm and the intercostal muscles are the chief agents of respiration. It must be reiterated, however, that local control cannot be exercised over them. But their reflexive behavior *can* be influenced by how the musculature that surrounds them is activated.

The Thorax

The degree of sternum elevation largely determines the posture of the chest cavity (the thorax). If the manubrium (the keystone and uppermost portion of the sternum) falls, the ribs and the chest also tend to collapse. On inhalation, the intercartilaginous intercostal muscles raise the ribs. These movements are influenced by the position of the sternum. In inhalation, the diaphragm descends slightly and presses the viscera forward, which produces a slight expansion of the frontal abdominal wall. The lower ribs are elevated and expanded and the volume of the lungs is increased. At inhalation a significant percentage of abdominal wall expansion is of an anterolateral nature (in front and to the sides) and at dorsal regions. In exhalation, the interosseus internal intercostals depress the ribs. But the singer can be taught to retain much of the inspiratory position over extended periods of time, so that the chest cavity need not rapidly collapse.

The Abdominal Musculature

Four broad flat muscles of the abdomen assist in maintaining a stable thoracic posture: (1) the transverse abdominis runs horizontally from the internal surface of the rib cage and crosses the torso; (2) the internal oblique muscles cross the abdomen; (3) the external oblique muscles cross the abdomen; and (4) the rectus abdominis provides an outer shield, and keeps the viscera in place. These strong abdominal muscles largely determine phrase lengths of the singing voice (fig. 3.1).

At the moment of inspiration, abdominal muscle groups are positioned in complementary relationships. They can be taught to retain inhalatory alliances for much longer periods of time than is experienced in normal

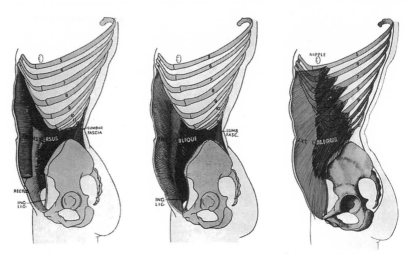

Figure 3.1. Abdominal musculature

speech. Such learned maneuvers heighten awareness of an age-old breath-management technique internationally known as the *appoggio.* On deep or complete inhalation, the muscles reach a fuller distention, a position that can be preserved in the inspiratory posture for a relatively extensive period of time.

Happily, the onset exercises that follow, and the development of "breath support" in singing, are reciprocal enterprises. One of the most effective methods for learning breath management for singing lies in the systematic application of rhythmic variations on the short basic onset exercise. At the moment of inhalation, a slight distention of the diaphragm occurs and, as fuller lung capacity is reached, the lateral-abdominal wall is expanded. The sternum must be maintained in a noble position, neither rising nor falling in either inhalation or exhalation. There must be no sensation of overcrowding the lungs.

Appoggio

The term appoggio derives from the verb *appoggiare,* which means to lean against, to be in contact with, or to support. As a pedagogic term, appoggio refers to contact among the muscles of inspiration at the moment of deep inhalation. A telling explanation of the appoggio came from Francesco Lamperti nearly 150 years ago: "The muscles of inspiration must not give up quickly to the muscles of expiration." In his *Treatise on the Art of Singing* (originally written in French), F. Lamperti described the appoggio action as *la lutte vocale* (the vocal contest):

To sustain a given note the air should be expelled slowly; to attain this end, the respiratory muscles, by continuing their action, retain the air in the lungs, and oppose their action to that of the expiratory muscles, which is called the lutte vocale, or vocal struggle. On the retention of this equilibrium depends the just emission of the voice, and by means of it alone can true expression be given to the sound produced.

The appoggio technique of breath management establishes a condition of dynamic equilibrium (as opposed to static positioning) among the muscles of the torso and thorax and the laryngeal musculature. This all-important muscular cooperation can be systematically drilled and extended for increasingly longer periods of time. Figure 3.1 illustrates the abdominal musculature involved in the appoggio technique, particularly the transversus abdominis, the obliquus internus abdominis, and the obliquus externus abdominis.

Alerting the Singer to the Appoggio Experience

Consonants bring about changes in the respiratory-articulatory mechanism. They affect the airflow rate and can be of assistance in establishing an awareness of the appoggio. We consider some examples.

EXERCISE 3.1

While phonating with a closed mouth, /m/ (the "hum") can be spread out over a number of seconds. Place the hands just below the ribcage, at the sides of the body, with the thumbs in the dorsal region at the twelfth rib, and the four fingers of each hand in contact with the sides of the lateral abdominal wall. Hum—at as high a dynamic level as possible—on single pitches in low and middle ranges. Note the muscle contact in the lateral and anterior abdominal wall.

[m]   [m]

Exercise 3.1

Produce reiterated siren-like impulses on the continuant /m/ executed on rising and falling pitch levels at relatively high dynamic levels.

This maneuver brings about an awareness of the increase in the abdominal-wall muscular activity involved with each new impulse. As the singer engages in each of the mounting pitch excursions, he will experience additional appoggio action, manifested by increased muscular activity both laterally and frontally in the area of the abdomen.

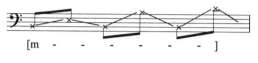

Exercise 3.2a

EXERCISES 3.2B AND C

The same results can be experienced by the use of the consonants /v/, and /z/, also executed in siren-like fashion. These voiced consonants result from precise occlusion (closure) of the vocal folds. The rate of airflow during a sustained phonation on /v/, and similarly on /z/, depends on the degree of appoggio activity and the extent of resistance to the exiting breath. Hands placed at the sides of the abdomen monitor the degree of resistance.

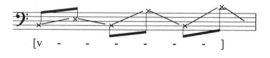

Exercise 3.2b

Exercise 3.2c

EXERCISE 3.3A

Because the velar consonant /k/ requires velopharyngeal closure of the tongue and the velum—the breath being momentarily inhibited from emission—responding sensations of contact can be felt in the muscles of the lateral-abdominal wall.

A repetition of the unvoiced phoneme /k/, within a single breath, also can alert the singer to lower-trunk involvement (the source of the appoggio, it must be kept in mind).

[k   k   k   k]

Exercise 3.3a

EXERCISE 3.3B

Reiterate a sustained phrase on the syllable /ke/ (and on syllables with other vowels that are prefaced by /k/), as in exercise 3.3b, without interruption from breath renewal. The combination of the unvoiced phoneme /k/ and the subsequent vowel also alerts a singer to the appoggio event.

Exercise 3.3b

EXERCISE 3.4

The sustained tongue-point trill (the rolled /r/) is another consonantal device that induces sensations of contact among muscles of the abdomen. In order to produce a sustained rolled /r/ over a few seconds, abdominal support must be experienced. The tongue-point trill also can be executed on a 5–4–3–2–1 pattern, or some other noncomplex scale combination.

Exercise 3.4

EXERCISE 3.5A

If the singer cannot execute a rolled /r/, rapid spoken repetition of the phrase "put-it-out" may induce related action that resembles the toungue-point trill.

EXERCISE 3.5B

Although not pertinent to generating sensations of the appoggio (the topic here under consideration), execution of the alveolar /r/ ("flipped r") may prove helpful to the American singer accustomed to regional speech patterns that habitually make use of the "retroflex r." By executing consecutively the name of the Italian city Bari and the English word "body," tongue action is assisted in proper execution of rapid single-tap /r/.

The singer should discover which of the following exercises brings about the greatest consciousness of the appoggio contact. Several nonpitch exercises have a long history of considerable value in alerting a singer to the appoggio phenomenon.

EXERCISE 3.6A

The slowly emitted sibilant /s/ is one of them. With the hands monitoring the sides of the abdomen, slowly emit a barely audible sibilant /s/ through a nearly closed mouth. As lung volume diminishes, there is awareness of changes in the epigastric and umbilical regions, but, with perseverance, the lateral abdominal posture remains admirably until the very end of the exercise.

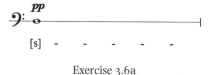

Exercise 3.6a

EXERCISE 3.6B

Another use of the sibilant /s/ produces a /s-s-s-s/ series, in rapid staccato fashion, consecutively executed on a single breath. There is a feeling of articulation in the abdominal area, but the ribcage retains its initial posture, without collapse.

Exercise 3.6b

A similar ancient device is the execution of a /f-f-f-f-f/ pattern, accomplished as though five candles were being blown out on a single breath emission. Feel centered epigastric/umbilical activity (the epigastrium lies just above the umbilical region), while at the same time the lateral abdominal wall retains its inspiratory posture. This technique resembles the earlier laughterlike onsets and the silent sibilant exercise.

[f - f - f - f - f   f - f - f - f - f   f - f - f - f - f]

Exercise 3.6c

EXERCISE 3.6D

A nonphonatory device is to pant rapidly, first audibly, then silently. Responses of the epigastrium and the abdominal wall induce articulatory motions while the torso remains in the inspiratory posture.

"Farinelli's Exercise"

Perhaps the most efficacious silent-breath exercise is popularly called "Farinelli's Exercise." The great eighteenth-century castrato Carlo Broschi was known as Farinelli. Despite the lack of supportive historical evidence, oral tradition has it that following the advice of his famous teacher, Nicola Porpora, Farinelli performed this silent exercise repeatedly each day. It will be recalled that Farinelli was called "the silent breather," and that because he could take such rapid, silent breath renewals, he gave the impression of being able to sustain phrases of unbelievable length.

FARINELLI'S EXERCISE (1)

The singer lies on his back. It is best that a pillow or two be placed under the head to ensure that the larynx is not elevated. Breathe normally, feeling as relaxed as possible. Place one hand on the front of the abdominal wall, the other at the side of the lower ribs. Notice the expansion that occurs at inhalation. Next, lengthen this inhalatory gesture, retaining it for as long as is comfortable.

There is no sensation of "holding the breath"; one simply suspends the respiratory process. Breathing should be quiet and regular.

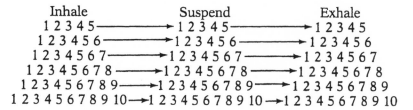

Figure 3.2. Farinelli pyramid chart (inhalation/suspension/exhalation)

Lips ought to be parted so that there is no holding back of the breath by the lips in the process. Aim for easy suspension of the breath, its measured exhalation, and for quiet breath renewal.

The Farinelli maneuver consists of three distinct but interrelated segments of the breath-cycle. The glottis remains open throughout the cycle. Never "hold the breath." Count mentally, or rhythmically tap out the counts, during each of the three phases of the silent breath-pacing maneuver.

1. Paced inhalation. Quietly inhale over a count of four.
2. Retention of the breath. Remain in the inhalation position for a count of four.
3. Regulation of the exit of the breath. Pace the exit of breath, without audible exhalation, over a count of four.

FARINELLI'S EXERCISE (2)

Gradually elongate the segments of the breath cycle, with silent renewal taken by the nose or through slightly parted lips. By sequentially increasing numbers, a count of ten seconds for each of the segments eventually becomes accomplishable during a single breath cycle of approximately forty seconds. No matter what the duration, each breath is complete but uncrowded. There is no sensation of stuffing the lungs with breath. In the expiration phase of the higher numbers, some minimal contraction of the abdomen may occur, but there is no sudden inward anterior-lateral collapsing or ribcage displacement. (At an appropriate moment, Farinelli's Exercise will be joined with singing and physical movement [see chapter 16]).

Vocalises must not long remain isolated from musical encounters. Principles of breath management have value only as they are applicable to what the singer encounters in performance. In transferring the appoggio principle from exercises to musical phrases, I find it useful to have the singer perform model phrases from the literature.

Although choosing from the song and operatic literatures becomes a somewhat arbitrary exercise, the baritone who is serious about achieving professional skills will find the excerpts listed below to be of value. Several short extracts should be made part of the daily breath-technique routine. A singer should choose from among them, varying the selection as he sees fit (see chapter 17).

Breath-Management Literature Examples for the Young Singer

English-Language Excerpts

Literature Example 3.1. *Samson,* Handel

Literature Example 3.2. "To One Unknown," Carpenter

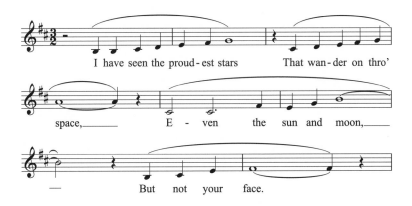

Literature Example 3.3. "Green River," Carpenter

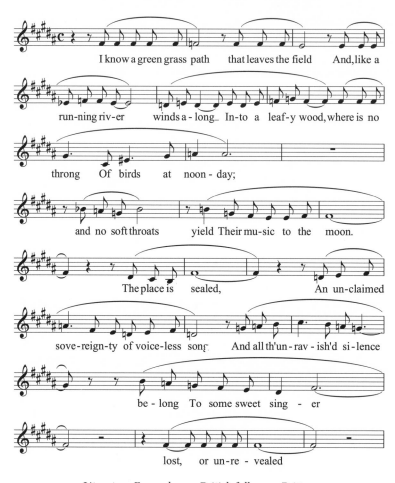

Literature Example 3.4. British folksong, Britten

(continued)

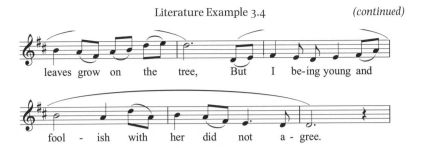

leaves grow on the tree, But I be-ing young and

fool – ish with her did not a – gree.

Literature Example 3.5. Hymn tune, Copland

Shall we gath-er by the ri – ver, Where bright an-gel feet have

trod,____ With its crys-tal tide for-ev – er Flow-ing

by the__ throne of__ God. Yes, we'll gath-er by the

riv – er, the beau-ti-ful, the beau-ti-ful riv – er,

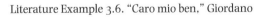

Gath – er with the saints by the riv – er That

flows by the throne of God.____

Italian-Language Excerpts

Literature Example 3.6. "Caro mio ben," Giordano

Ca – ro mio ben, cre – di-mi al-men, sen – za di

te lan – gui-sce il cor,

Literature Example 3.7. "Selve amiche," Caldara

Sel - ve a - mi - che, om - bro - se pian - te, fi - do al - ber - go del mio co - - - - re, fi - do al - ber - - - - - - - go del mio co - - re,

Literature Example 3.8. "Come raggio di sol," Caldara

Co - me rag - gio di sol mi - te e se - re - no, co - me rag - gio di sol mi - te e se - re - no sov - ra pla - ci - di flut - ti si ri - po - sa, men - tre del ma - re, men - tre del ma - re nel pro - fon - do se - no sta la tem - pe - - sta a - sco - sa:

Literature Example 3.9. "Pietà, Signore," Stradella

Pie - tà, Si - gno - re, di me do - len - te! Si - gnor, pie - tà, se a te giun - ge il mi - o pre - gar; Non mi pu - ni - sca il tu - o ri - gor,

Literature Example 3.10. *Don Giovanni*, Mozart

Deh, vie - ni al - la fi - ne - stra, o mi - o te -
so - ro. Deh, vie - ni a con - so - lar il pian - to mi - o.
Se ne - ghi a me di dar qual - che ri - sto -
ro, da - van - ti a - gli oc - chi tuoi mo - rir vo - gl'i - o.

French-Language Excerpts

Literature Example 3.11. "Bois épais," Lully

Bois é - pais re - dou - ble ton om - bre,
Tu ne sau - rais être as - sez som - bre, Tu ne peux trop ca -
cher Mon mal - heur - eux a - mour, Je sens un des - es - poir Dont l'hor -
reur est ex - trê - me, Je ne dois plus voir ce que
j'ai - me, Je ne veux plus souf - frir le jour.

Literature Example 3.12. "Ici-bas," Fauré

I - ci-bas tous les li-las meu-rent, Tous les chants des oi-seaux sont

courts, Je rè - ve aux é - tés qui de-meu-rent tou - jours!

Literature Example 3.13. "Lydia," Fauré

Ly-di-a sur tes ro-ses jou - es Et sur ton col frais et si blanc.

Roule é - tin-ce-lant L'or flu - i - de que tu dé-nou - es;

Literature Example 3.14. "Nell," Fauré

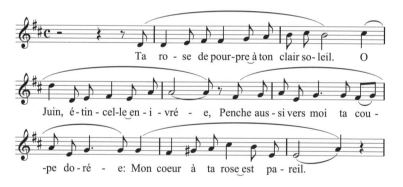

Ta ro - se de pour-pre à ton clair so- leil. O

Juin, é - tin - cel-le en - i - vré - e, Penche aus - si vers moi ta cou -

-pe do - ré - e: Mon coeur à ta rose est pa - reil.

German-Language Excerpts

Literature Example 3.15. "An die Musik," Schubert

Du hol-de Kunst, in wie-viel grau-en Stun-den, wo mich des
Le - bens wil - der Kreis um - strickt,
hast du mein Herz zu war - mer Lieb ent -
zun - den, hast mich in ei - ne beß - re Welt ent -
rückt, in ei - ne beß - re Welt ent- rückt!

Literature Example 3.16. "Litanei," Schubert

Ruhn in Frie-den al - le See - len, die voll-bracht ein
ban - ges Quä- len, die voll - en - det sü - ßen Traum,
le-bens-satt, ge-bo-ren kaum, aus der Welt hin-ü - ber- schie-den:
Al - le See - len ruhn in Frie - den!

Literature Example 3.17. "Der Nussbaum," Schumann

Es grü-net ein Nuß-baum vor dem Haus,

duf-tig, luf - tig brei-tet er blätt-rig die Blät-ter aus.

Viel lieb - li - che Blü - ten ste - hen d'ran;

lin - de Win - de kom - men, sie herz - lich zu um-fahn.

Literature Example 3.18. "Im Rhein, im schönen Strome," Liszt

Im Rhein, im schö - nen Stro - me, da spie-gelt sich in den

Wel - len, mit sei - nem gro - ßen Do - me,

das gro - ße, das heil' - ge Köln.

In each excerpt, the aim is to manage silent breath preparation at the phrase onset, retention of the inspiratory posture during phrase execution, and silent breath renewal at termination of the phrase. In essence, the Farinelli maneuver is now directly applied to the performance material. In some instances, the pauses between phrases indicate slowly paced inhalation; in other cases, cumulative phrases require immediate breath renewal.

Chapter 4

VOWEL DEFINITION
AND THE *CHIAROSCURO*

The Role of Spectral Analysis

No artist has ever learned to sing by studying a spectrogram of his own voice or of the voices of great artists, by analyzing formant relationships, or by determining what mouth postures best track which vowels. One learns to sing only by developing a tonal concept and by establishing a daily routine for its achievement (see chapters 13 and 17).

Yet spectrographic analysis can reveal factors that heighten a singer's awareness of what makes for completeness of tonal resonance. Acoustic analysis can show nothing that the cultivated ear cannot hear, but it can confirm and secure what the cultivated ear recognizes. For some singers and their teachers, there remains a hesitancy to examine spectrally the sounds of singing, out of fear that it might reveal errors best ignored, or that analysis might turn the creative art into something mechanistic and devoid of individuality. On the contrary, I have yet to meet any apprentice singer or professional artist who has not been fascinated to see what his or her sound looks like, and who has not wished to examine the usable colors of the voice; nor have I yet encountered any person who could not readily fully comprehend the user-friendly graphs within minutes. Indeed, it is easier for most of us to learn to read spectrum analysis than it was to learn to read the bass clef. It is not the aim of spectral analysis to bring about general uniformity of timbre from singer to singer but to determine what constitutes the individual's best sound and to stabilize it. Despite wide diversities within the field of voice pedagogy, there is general agreement on the qualities that make up elite vocalism. These characteristics are mostly expressed in subjective terms that are often considered inappropriate by members of the scientific community but are completely understandable to professional voice practitioners. Such practical expressions include "warmth," "depth," "roundness," "velvet," "vitality," "ring," "ping," "focus," "placement," "point," and "balance." Every professional singer who is aware of the complete singing tone (*voce completa*) strives for these features.

A spectrogram provides graphic, visual representations of the harmonic components of vocalized sound. At playback, one can *see* as well as *hear* the sounds of singing. (For a fuller exposition, refer to "Spectrographic Analysis of the Singing Voice," *On the Art of Singing*, R. Miller, 1996, 275–280.) Increasingly, university schools of music and conservatories recognize that spectral analysis is a valuable adjunct to the teaching of singing. By comparing the various timbres he is capable of making, a singer is empowered to visualize which sounds represent his fully resonant tone and to determine what may be lacking.

The Vowel Series and Their Formants

Phoneticians speak of a front-vowel (lateral) series /i–ɪ–e–ɛ–æ/ and of a back-vowel (rounded) series /ɑ–o–ʊ–u/. The classic front-to-back vowel progression is /i–e–ɑ–o–u/. A vowel is classified by the positioning of the tongue body during its execution, action that happens below the level of conscious control. In the front-vowel sequence, the anterior portion of the tongue approaches the hard palate, and the posterior portion of the tongue is lowered. In the back-vowel series, the anterior portion of the tongue is lowered and the back portion of the tongue is raised toward the soft palate. Spectral analysis reveals the resonance distinctiveness of any spoken or sung phonation. Figure 4.1 indicates a spectrographic display of a series of vowels in lower-middle range, sung by a professional operatic male voice. Three parameters provide in-

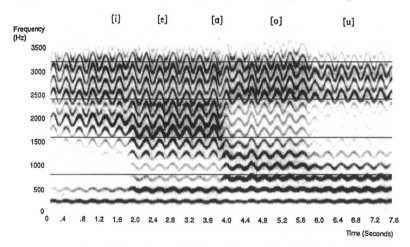

Figure 4.1. Spectral display of the diagonal cardinal-vowel sequence sung in mid-low range by a professional operatic male voice

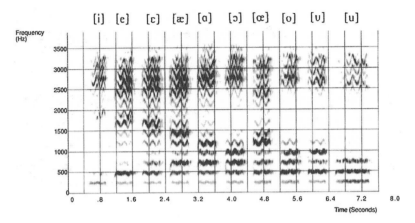

Figure 4.2. Spectral display of a series of vowels sung in mid-low range by a professional operatic male voice

formation: (1) the horizontal axis represents time; (2) the left axis represents frequency (the number of vibrations per second by which pitch is determined); and (3) the degree of darkness indicates the strength of the harmonic partials (overtones) that are multiples of the fundamental-frequency rate of vibration.

Formants are regions of strong acoustic energy that determine the characteristics of spoken or sung vowels. The first formant occupies the lower regions of the graph. Together with the fundamental, it supplies the "depth" of the sound. In response to physical alterations in the vocal tract, the second formant shifts appropriately as vowel definition changes. Thus, together with the first formant, the second formant indicates the location of acoustic strength associated with a particular vowel (figure 4.1).

Figure 4.1 shows the progression of vowel differentiation in an /i–e–a–o–u/ sequence. The steplike progression from /i/ to /u/ is termed the sequential vowel diagonal. (The waviness in the spectra displays the phenomenon of vibrato.)

Figure 4.2 extends the vowel sequence to /i–e–ɛ–æ–a–ɔ–œ–o–ʊ–u/.

The Singer's Formant

The phonation of a trained singer displays a heightened phenomenon known as "the singer's formant" (the third formant) that corresponds to the subjective terms "ring," "ping," or "forward placement" mentioned earlier. Observable in the upper region of the spectrum, the third formant occurs in the baritone voice in the region of 2800Hz to 3200Hz, in the bass-baritone around 2600Hz to 2800Hz, and for the bass at roughly 2400Hz to 2600Hz. William Vennard (1967) termed this acoustic strength "the 2800 factor."

It is currently held that the lower airway segment (epilaryngeal tube) of the vocal tract is the probable source of the singer's formant. The distribution of acoustic energy in the upper, middle, and lower portions of the spectrum determines the acoustic balance of a vowel. The singer's formant is also present in the male voice in much of supported speech.

As early as 1942, pioneer researcher Wilmer T. Bartholomew described the singer's formant in *The Acoustics of Music*. Ralph D. Appelman, noted bass-baritone and researcher, directed attention to the third formant in his 1967 *The Science of Vocal Pedagogy*. Johan Sundberg brought the topic to prominence in his seminal 1974 *The Acoustics of the Singing Voice*. A number of contemporary writers point out its importance in elite vocalism (see the select bibliography).

"Voice Placement"

International subjective expressions have long described the desirable distribution of acoustic energy. Italians call it "*l'imposto*" (or "*l'impostazione della voce*"). French singers speak of "*placement*," Germans of "*Sitz*," and English-speaking singers refer to "the placement of the voice." In point of fact, tone cannot be "placed" in any location. It is already roughly 1,100 feet beyond its producer before he becomes aware of it. Proprioceptive reactions to resonator adjustment bring about the perception of "voice placement." The sensations of "placement" are caused by sympathetic vibration conducted by the bony structures of the chest or head. In historic voice pedagogy, the singer's formant remains constant, regardless of register transitions, dynamic levels, or velocity.

As noted earlier, traditional voice pedagogy identifies three registers: *voce di petto* ("chest"); (2) *voce mista* ("mixed voice"); and (3) *voce di testa*, also termed *voce piena in testa* ("full head voice"). Other identifiable timbres are *voce finta* (feigned voice), and *falsetto* (the imitative sound of the female voice produced by the male). The chiaroscuro, which testifies to the presence of the singer's formant, ought to be common to all of them. (Premier countertenors learn to bring the singer's formant into falsetto timbre.)

Voce finta

Before turning to a discussion of the chiaroscuro tone, let us briefly consider the quality known as voce finta. Freely translated, voce finta means "feigned voice." It is not identical to falsetto, because in finta quality the vocal folds are fully approximated, whereas in normal male falsetto there is somewhat less firm closure of the voice folds (see chapter 10). Because vocal-fold occlusion resembles that of voce piena (full, or complete, voice), voce finta can readily be turned into voce piena without noticeable alteration in quality. It is produced by a slight elevation of the larynx and by a reduction in breath energy. The finta timbre tends to some extent to employ an ethereal, disembodied nature and is useful as a rare vocal coloration but not as a standard timbre. Voce finta quality should be used sparingly. Never should it serve as a substitute for true piano dynamic level. One hears its effective use in such low-voiced male singers as Robert Merrill, Leonard Warren, Dietrich Fischer-Dieskau, Gérard Souzay, Thomas Quasthoff, Dmitri Hvorostovsky, Thomas Hampson, and other current leading performers.

Securing the Chiaroscuro Tone

Problems that plague many singers (including some who are professionally successful) often happen because of maladjustments in the resonator tract, particularly of the lips, tongue, jaw, or pharynx. Depending on the ease of production, a singer may need to consider only a few of the suggested corrective devices that follow. A second singer may be in need of most of them. The accomplished singer most likely has already attained lip, tongue, jaw and throat freedom, but if problems remain, he is well advised to consider these suggestions. Functional contributions of the individual parts of the vocal tract are considered here.

The Role of the Tongue

The chief vector of the vocal tract is the tongue. Fortunately, the vocal tract of Homo sapiens is constructed so as to allow production of speech sounds not available to the higher apes, and possibly not available to man's early relative, Neanderthal man (Lieberman, Philip, and E. S. Crelin, 1971).

The tongue, attached to the hyoid bone, extends forward to the lips, occupying most of the vocal tract—the resonator tube that extends from the larynx to the lips. (The hyoid is a U-shaped bone from which the larynx is suspended; the vocal tract is the chief resonator of the singing voice.) The shapes assumed by the tongue determine spatial arrangements of the vocal-resonation system.

Using the Front and Back Vowel Series

As previously indicated, with the front (lateral) vowel series the forward portion of the tongue is in various degrees of elevation toward the hard palate, whereas in the back (rounded) vowel series the tongue is elevated in its posterior portion toward the soft palate. The lateral positions of the mouth, lip, and jaw are favorable to the resonance balance of the front vowels, which are strong in upper harmonics.

In front-vowel formations, particularly in the speech-inflection range, the pharynx is given preference as resonator (because the mouth is positioned in narrower shapes). The mouth is capable of opening gradually in the ascending scale without obliterating front-vowel definition. By contrast, during the production of back vowels, the mouth becomes the chief resonator because it grows more spacious through jaw lowering and by tongue flattening. In speech, the formants of the voice lower during the progression from lateral to rounded vowels. However, in order to avoid tensions, the blade or apex (front perimeter) of the tongue should remain in contact with the inner surface of the lower front teeth for all vowels—whether back or front—and for approximately 70 percent of all consonant production as well. Lingual flexibility so essential to vocal freedom is thereby assured.

Inasmuch as the tongue is the frequent source of tension in faultily sung tone, natural articulation of spoken vowels may help to establish greater tongue freedom. With the cardinal vowels /i–e–ɑ–o–u/, spoken slowly, the singer becomes aware of direct contact of the tongue with the inner surface of the lower front teeth (as mentioned earlier). This is the case for each of the vowels, from the most lateral vowel /i/ to the most rounded vowel /u/.

Several defective tendencies are common among low-voiced males during the sustaining of a single vowel or in a series of vowel changes: (1) drawing the tongue back into a retroflex posture; (2) raising the apex of the tongue toward the hard palate; (3) placing the tip of the tongue below the roots of the lower front teeth; (4) curling the sides of the tongue away from contact with the teeth, which humps up its midsection; and (5) turning the tongue slightly to left or right in unnatural positions. These errors generally take place together with an exaggerated dropped mandible (jaw).

EXERCISE 4.1

The use of a hand mirror to observe the exact location of the tongue blade (which should remain identical in speech and in singing) proves an invaluable aid. As a corrective procedure, speak the /i–e–ɑ–o–u/ vowel sequence on a pitch in a comfortable range. Then sing the same sequence on single pitches in the speech-inflection region, using the hand mirror to monitor both speaking and singing. The postures of the lips and the jaw will alter minimally, but the tongue tip stays in its permanent forward location. As pitch ascends, the mouth may open slightly more, but tongue positions (determined by the vowel) remain intact.

Exercise 4.1

Using Consonant Pairs to Induce
Correct Tongue Postures

Some consonants are partnered as voiced or unvoiced pairs, connoting phonetic production of parallel physical and acoustic action. For the voiced consonants, the vocal folds are approximated. The vocal folds remain unoccluded for the unvoiced consonants. Some of the pedagogically useful combination pairs are:

Voiced	Unvoiced
b	p
d	t
v	f
g	k
s	z

To gain tongue freedom and to establish the proper resonance spaces in the mouth and the pharynx, preface the vowel with a voiced consonant, then alternate it with its unvoiced consonant mate. The tongue apex remains at rest at the inner surface of the lower front teeth. Patterns on any number of notes can be devised, and the few given here are but samples of the possibilities. For example, begin with a simple 1–2–3–2–1 pattern in speaking range, prefacing each note on the lateral vowel /e/ with the voiced consonant /b/ (exercise 4.2).

EXERCISE 4.2

Make certain that the tongue retains the same location for the vowel as it had for the consonant. The lips will open slightly during the progression from the consonant to the vowel, but there is no excessive jaw movement. See that the anterior portion of the tongue stays relaxed against the inner surface of the lower front teeth.

Exercise 4.2

EXERCISE 4.3

Next, use the unvoiced paired consonant /p/ in similar fashion (exercise 4.3).

Exercise 4.3

EXERCISE 4.4

Extend the maneuver to a quickly executed 5–4–3–2–1 pattern. All voiced and unvoiced pairs can be alternately applied. A favorite combination of mine is the /v–f/ pair, which makes evident the contact of the tongue with the inner surface of the lower front teeth. In all cases, diphthongization of the vowel conclusion should be avoided.

Exercise 4.4

EXERCISE 4.5

After flexible tongue action has been established, couple the bilabial pilot consonant /b/ with a consonant that is formed at the alveolar ridge, such as /r/ and /l/.

Exercise 4.5

EXERCISE 4.6

Determine that the tongue, during the execution of consonants /v/, /l/, or /r/, does not linger in a transitory posture but makes a quick return to its proper position for formation of the vowel.

Exercise 4.6

More on the Retroflex Tongue

I have cited the need for the tongue to be in contact with the inner surface of the lower front teeth for all vowels and for most consonants. A problematic deviation for many baritones, bass-baritones, and basses comes from the retroflex tongue. For most North Americans (and for those Europeans who have learned their English pronunciation from American television), the so-called Midwestern /r/ carries over into the singing voice. This is a circumstance in which the classically trained singer must not sing as he speaks, because the retroflex tongue posture is not sustainable without tension in the tongue and jaw. (The retroflex-tongue Midwestern /r/ as spoken by most North Americans is clearly illustrated in the first line of the biblical "Lord's Prayer"—"Our father who art in heaven.") Only in musical theater, folk singing, contemporary Christian, and popular commercial arts is the retroflex-tongue posture acceptable.

The duration factor (greater elongation in song than in speech) makes the retroflex /r/ less tenable during singing than in speech. With some singers, the tongue remains in the retroflex position throughout both the consonant /r/ and subsequent vowel, to the general detriment of vocal freedom.

There is also the problem of the tongue assuming a retroflex position for vowels sung in high ranges, in which case the spatial relationships of the separate divisions (mouth and pharynx) of the buccopharyngeal cavity are unfavorably rearranged, with tension replacing freedom. Voice teachers in general are committed to tongue freedom, but how that freedom is to be arrived at varies from technique to technique. Inventive and counterproductive recommendations consist of placing lozenges, coins, marbles, or other objects, on the tongue, a utensil (such as the spoon) to depress the tongue, and admonitions to hold the tongue in a constantly low, grooved position throughout the vowel series, regardless of the vowel being sung. Other suggestions include manually pulling the apex of the tongue forward, distending the tongue out of the mouth, or holding the tongue apex with a handkerchief while producing sound. Having observed the demonstration of these devices in various studios, it is my viewpoint that such measures are excessive, and that they produce unwanted results. They clearly are in conflict with front-vowel/back-vowel phonetic function.

When one thinks aloud, as when saying "uh-yes," or makes pensive affirmation in the major foreign languages common to elite singing, the tongue and the vocal tract lie in a neutral posture, represented by the phoneme /ə/. The same position is present when one says "Um-hm!" The use of a hand mirror will help overcome the problem of the retroflex tongue. Incidentally, the mirror is your finest teacher, and by far the most economical!

The Role of the Jaw

Some sources go so far as to advocate that the jaw ought to remain in a single low position and that the tongue must learn to adjust to jaw immobility. Some teachers actually recommend retaining "the idiot jaw." A commonly heard admonition is "open the throat by dropping the jaw," a favorite device of certain choral conductors who want to establish uniform timbre across a diverse group of voices. The problem is that dropping the jaw does not open the throat. It simply gives preference to the mouth to the detriment of balanced mouth/pharynx resonances. Greater prominence of mouth resonance tends to uniformly lower the formants of the voice.

The pharynx can be widened when the mouth is closed. (To prove the point, yawn with the lips occluded.) Although the jaw lowers when one laughs uproariously or cries aloud with grief, the zygomatic facial muscles are not pulled downward. The position of the jaw should be in accordance with natural vowel definition, in all ranges, and at all dynamic levels.

The Role of the Facial Elevator Muscles

Every singer eventually learns that teachers of singing are divided into distinct camps with regard to what should be done with the musculature of the face. In one approach, the upper lip is pulled downward and smiling is always to be avoided. Others, as we have seen, believe in the rubric "*si canta come si parla.*" This latter group encourages the retention of a pleasant facial expression. Which of these positions can be justified by what is knowable about acoustics and physiology? Essential information on the relationships of acoustics and physiology as they relate to the art of singing demands a brief digression.

The zygomatic arch is a bony structure that extends from the cheeks to the anterior sides of the skull. The zygomatic bone itself lends definition to the facial structure. Zygomatic muscles consist of slender bands on either side of the face; they rise from the zygomatic bone and insert into the skin at the corners of the mouth; they lodge at the maxilla, the area between the lips and the cheeks. Major and minor zygomatic muscles are among muscle groups that determine the movement of the fascia, thereby controlling alterations in facial expression. Zygomaticus major inserts into the angles of the mouth. Fibers of the levator anguli oris, the orbicularis oris (a muscle that encircles the mouth), and the risorious (smiling) muscles, define pleasant emotional states. Slight elevation of the zygomatic muscles accompanies ease and comfort.

The facial elevator muscles are crucial to resonator-tract shape and determine the facial expressions of normal communication. Facial muscle groups can remain somewhat elevated, no matter the emotional content. Contrariwise, the depressor muscles counter the elevator muscles by pulling the lips and the mouth downward. In some systems of singing, even the grimacing muscle—the platysma muscle—is activated, with the shape of the vocal tract adversely affected. In conjunction with the lips and the jaw, positions of the facial muscles can be neutral, dropped, or elevated. What works best for singing?

Slight elevation of the zygomatic muscles is characteristic of most major singing artists, including low-voiced males. When a pleasant facial expression is present at the moment of full inhalation, the velum may even rise slightly, enhancing the shape of the buccopharyngeal resonator tube. The positions of the zygomatic muscles and the upper lip help determine the shapes assumed by the buccal-pharyngeal cavity. Normal communicative facial expressions—neither mugging nor grinning—have a favorable effect on the resonator tract, and contribute to the art of communication. Fixated facial musculatures do not enhance the quality of the singing tone.

A widely dispersed traditional pedagogy advocates "singing in the masque," "placing the tone in the masque," or "directing the breath into the masque." As has been proven physiologically, it is not possible to "place" either sound or exiting air. Yet the singer experiences sensations in the forward portion of his face that he associates with the location of sound (see chapter 12). Excessive concentration on lifting the zygomatic arch and on retaining the full smile position results in overly bright, shrill timbre. Lateral vowels encourage an upward lift of the facial musculature. By retaining the lateral smile position for all vowels, the zygomatic muscles are placed in an unnatural "grinning" posture for the entire vowel sequence.

The risorius (smiling muscle) is a paired narrow band of muscle fibers that rises from the fascia over the masseters (chewing muscles). A muscle of the cheek, risorius inserts into tissue at the corners of the mouth. Although related, the two muscle groups (zygomatic and risorius) are capable of independent action. There can be a pleasant look on the face—activity of the zygomatic muscles—without full participation of the risorius muscles. However, in ascending pitch, if there is no adjustment of the lateral (front) vowel so as to produce vowel modification, a strident top register will result. Vowel integrity can be maintained while the facial musculature retains some degree of elevation, yet the jaw must appropriately open as the zona di passaggio and the secondo passaggio are reached.

The jaw generally lowers in yawning and snoring; neither is appropriate to the vitality demanded by the act of singing. Unfortunately, some singers seem to have been caught in a permanent gaping posture. The jaw assumes a fully dropped posture in regurgitation, at which time the mouth opens widely and the vocal tract is closed off so that the bolus can be expelled by way of the esophagus. If the mouth is opened in similar fashion for singing, it becomes the chief resonator, and contribution of the pharynx diminishes. Chiaroscuro balance is distorted. Oscuro aspects then clearly outweigh those of chiaro, and the tonal balance is upset. The vibrato rate becomes oscillatory (the pitch variant is too wide and too slow), and the timbre dull and weighty. As with all technical considerations, the guiding principle regarding mouth postures during singing should be "nothing in excess."

The Role of the Larynx
as a Resonator

The larynx is often overlooked as a resonator. The ventricular sinuses, also known as the sinuses of Morgagni or the laryngeal sinuses, lie between the false and true vocal folds. They are believed to play a significant role in producing the light/dark (chiaroscuro) timbre and indirectly contribute to the complete sound of the singer's formant in the professional singing voice (see chapter 16).

Although intrinsic laryngeal adjustments are below the level of a singer's control, the resonation factors of the larynx are mentioned here in order to avoid the error of attempting direct laryngeal control. A wise singer will not be preoccupied with what goes on in his larynx. The larynx undergoes a synergistic response to the vocal tract's resonation syndrome. Unfortunately, there are instructors who maintain that the intrinsic muscles of the larynx can be individually developed by specific maneuvers. Attempts at direct control over laryngeal function are among the most deadly of pedagogic sins.

Dealing with Tension in the Lips,
the Jaw, the Tongue, and the Neck

Consonants have already been considered as adjustors of the vocal tract in relation to breath-management. However, tension that is unrelated to airflow often specifically manifests itself in the lips, the jaw, the tongue, or the neck.

Freedom of the Lips

The vocal tract, as we have seen, extends from the internal laryngeal lips (the vocal folds) to the external lips. A currently fashionable exercise called the lip trill (lip bubble) supposedly relaxes the lips. But the lips are not tensed when the mouth is in normal phonatory postures. Lip tension occurs chiefly when singers try to fashion them in trumpet-like formations. In the absence of rigidity of the jaw and the tongue, the lips feel perfectly relaxed.

I find the popular lip trill to be mostly a superfluous activity. There is no hard evidence that it develops the vocal ligament or that it extends high and low ranges, as is at times claimed. In fairness, however, the lip trill does induce a certain degree of awareness of breath connection, and it may have psychological value. My main reservation about reliance on the lip trill is that it may act as a substitute for more productive maneuvers. It has become a downright menace in music-school hallways! Lip trilling is no surrogate for the practice room.

Tensions of the jaw, the tongue, and the neck often go together. Keeping the proper alignment of the head/neck/shoulder as a unit does much to eliminate above-the-torso stress. In most cases of head/neck/shoulder conflict, a few simple physical checks can prove corrective.

Freedom of the Larynx and the Jaw

Either distending or elevating the jaw moves the larynx away from its normal phonatory location. As has been seen, there is a tendency on the part of the male to raise his head and his larynx, as in calling, at the primo passaggio (see chapter 9). The stabilized larynx (with minimal articulatory movement) precludes this problem. If the singer has a tendency to elevate or thrust the jaw forward, the following exercises make that apparent.

EXERCISE 4.7. LATERAL MOVEMENT OF THE JAW

While keeping the head in a straightforward position, gently move the jaw from side to side. Continue to do so while singing a familiar phrase. Stop the motion but continue to sing. The same jaw looseness must remain.

EXERCISE 4.8. CROSSED PALMS ON THE ANTERIOR SKULL

The singer stands erect in a coordinated axial position. The palms of the hands, with intertwined fingers, rest on the forward top of the head. The head is poised at the axial position: the front of the neck feels short; the back of the neck feels long. Gently pressing the hands on the head, sing a phrase that ascends through the passaggio region, being careful to avoid thrusting the chin forward or raising the larynx. Then sing the same passage without the hand check.

EXERCISE 4.9. HAND PLACED ON THE OCCIPITAL BONE

In a related exercise, place the flat palm of one hand on the occipital bone (at the base of the skull), being certain to retain an axial posture. Ensure that the head does not elevate during the singing of an ascending scale.

EXERCISE 4.10. SECURING LARYNGEAL POSTURE BY MONITORING THE MANDIBULAR JOINT

It is a misguided concept to disjoint the jaw from the skull, as recommended by some pedagogies. By placing the little finger of each hand at the joint of the mandible while singing—with the rest of the fingers at the mastoid and the sides of the neck—the singer will verify that, even in hilarious high-pitched laughter (as well as in weeping), with the mouth fully opened, the jaw does not fall from its socket. During singing, the mandible should never be dislodged from its joint at the skull. First sing passages, monitoring to see that the jaw does not unhinge; repeat without the check.

EXERCISE 4.11. JAW CRADLING IN THE HAND

While cradling the jaw in one hand, sing a phrase while making certain that the chin and jaw are not thrust upward, downward, or forward.

Freedom of the Neck

Neck tension can result from a lack of external-frame support caused by elevation or forward posturing of the chin. The devices previously mentioned, applied to jaw tensions, can be directed to problems of neck tension.

EXERCISE 4.12. RELAXING THE NECK THROUGH MOVEMENT

While singing a phrase, turn the neck and head gently from side to side, making certain to maintain a poised sternum and torso. Movement must be lateral, never up and down. Then sing the phrase without the gesture.

Freedom of the Tongue

EXERCISE 4.13. LATERAL TONGUE MOVEMENT

While singing a single vowel in the comfortable speech-inflection range, slowly move the apex of the tongue from side to side across the inner surface of the lower front teeth. Then discontinue the movement while singing.

Freedom of the Pharynx

In optimal resonance balancing, what should be the function of the pharynx? I have reiterated that the vocal tract—chiefly comprising the mouth and the pharynx—is the main resonator of the voice. How much conscious control of the pharynx should a singer exercise? Are there safe techniques for manipulating the pharynx? Answers to these questions set voice pedagogies at odds with each other.

The vocal tract is a unified chamber that includes the nasopharynx, the oropharynx, and the laryngopharynx. Behind the nose lies the nasopharynx, lodged above the velum. Part of the oropharynx is visible when one looks at the back of the throat wall with a mirror and opens the mouth widely, while sustaining the exclamation "Ah!" An examiner sees the faucial isthmus, the passage situated between the velum and the base of the tongue. Visible in part to the eye are the pillars of the fauces, two muscular folds that form the narrow passage from the mouth to the pharynx. The soft palate—from which the uvula dangles—is capable of maintaining an open port or of accomplishing velar-pharyngeal closure. During normal voicing, the port is closed for all but nasal sounds (see chapter 16).

The lowest and externally invisible portion of the pharynx, known as the laryngopharynx, is located at the level of the larynx. The mouth and pharynx (buccopharyngeal resonator chamber) are connected by the oropharyngeal isthmus. Can these areas of the vocal tract be separately controlled as is suggested by several pedagogies?

Pharyngeal sensation and how it should be controlled in singing was long not uniform from one national culture to another. A major portion of the historic German School owed allegiance to a technique that aimed to create "chambers" and "domes" in the pharynx. This group of teachers proposed that pharyngeal space can be increased through conscious spreading of the pharyngeal wall, as in yawning. They were committed to conscious pharyngeal spreading. The singer was urged to imagine space in the throat that could accommodate an egg, an apple, a banana, or some such object. Fortunately, a number of internationally minded teachers of the modern German School have abandoned the spread-pharynx philosophy. They agree with the international school, which holds that the consciously spread pharynx produces a vocal *Knödel*—"a dumpling in the throat." Most cultivated listeners perceive Knödel timbre as being undesirably "pharyngeal."

In opposition to the spread pharynx tenet, mainstream historic pedagogy (the current international norm) never conceived of the pharynx as an independent resonator; the pharynx was considered part of the total buccopharyngeal resonance system.

If one breathes deeply and silently through the nose, the pharynx assumes the proper spatial arrangements for singing, without the necessity for additional rearrangement. At inhalation, there is a slight laryngeal descent and an increased sensation of spaciousness in the pharynx. This feeling may resemble a gentle incipient yawn but must never extend to the full-blown yawn. Indeed, the feeling of spaciousness may be related more to the posterior nasal and oropharynx areas of the vocal tract than to the region of the laryngopharynx.

As is the case with all pedagogic issues, satisfactory answers to questions regarding these opposing viewpoints can be found in the natural events of acoustics and physiology. When the complete yawn develops, the larynx is lowered to its fullest extent. It can only be retained in that low posture by the active participation of the depressor muscles of the larynx. Although the laryngeal/pharyngeal portions of the vocal tract also indicate some enlargement (when the larynx is depressed), if the pharynx is rigidly held in a distended posture, coordination among the three parts of the pharynx mentioned above is inhibited. Fluoroscopic and radiological examination of professional singers as they perform in various ranges show that when the larynx remains stable (relatively low), and when the articulatory actions of jaw, lips, tongue, and velum are permitted their natural processes, there is no single fixated pharyngeal position (see chapter 9). The pharynx engages in teamwork, along with the other members of the vocal tract, in a dynamic, nonstatic way.

Using the Nasal Continuants in Balancing the Chiaroscuro

Just as the nonnasal consonants assist in establishing proper resonance balance, so do the nasal continuants. We have seen the use of the sustained /m/ as a means for inducing appoggio awareness. The hum is acknowledged in all national and international pedagogies as a valuable aid in establishing good resonance balances in the singing voice, and with good reason.

The several forms of the nasal phonemes include: /m/ a bilabial nasal, /n/ an alveolar nasal, /ɲ/ a palatal nasal, and /ŋ/ a velar nasal. All four nasals promote acoustic energy in desirable parts of the spectrum: (1) the lower portion of the spectrum that indicates the combining of the fundamental with the first formant; (2) the middle portion of the spectrum that reveals the region of vowel definition; and (3) the upper spectral region that shows where the singer's formant lodges, and the extent to which the upper harmonic partials (overtones) coalesce. The nasals lend a hand as natural inducers for bringing about the resonance balance that produces the chiaroscuro tone.

Each of the four nasals incites specific sensations in the regions of the masque and the head. For most singers, /m/ feels more directly located on and around the lips. The phoneme /n/ seems to resound somewhat higher in the masque area. With /ɲ/, awareness is centered more completely in the masque. The nasal continuant /ŋ/ appears for most singers to lodge even higher in the head. As we have seen, each of these sensations is a result of sympathetic vibration in the bony structures of the face, not because tone or air has been *sent* to those locations. It is easy to mistake nasality for desirable resonance balance. A danger lies in striving for too strong a perception of the forward sensation of sound, thus causing excessive brightness or shrillness—an overbalance of upper harmonics (see chapter 16).

Pedagogies that allege voice resonance is best achieved by giving predominance to the nose and to the cavities of the head are examples of how faulty assumptions can induce disproportion among resonance components. In attempting to place the tone "forward," the role of the pharynx is diminished and the timbre becomes thin and incomplete. The core or center of the sound—the chiaroscuro—is depleted.

Slowly speak each of the four nasals as it occurs in the model words found in exercise 4.14.

EXERCISE 4.14

/m/ as in "my"

/n/ as in "no"

/ɲ/ as in "onion," "*ogni*," or "*agneau*"

/ŋ̩/ as in "song"

Then sustain them as sung phonations at comfortable pitch levels. Be aware of the accompanying sensations of sympathetic vibration in the face and head.

Consider each of the first three nasals in turn:

1. In the phoneme /m/ the lips are closed, but the nasal cavity, the mouth, the pharynx, and the larynx jointly act as resonators.
2. In the phoneme /n/ the apex of the tongue is in contact with the alveolar ridge (where the upper front teeth arise at the gum level) so that approximately one-third of frontal mouth resonance is removed. The remaining mouth resonance is conjoined with the nasal cavity, the pharynx and the larynx.
3. With the phoneme /ɲ/, the body of the tongue approaches the hard palate, which action cuts off about half of the mouth as a resonator. Full participation of the nasal cavity, the pharynx, and the larynx are retained. (It is impossible to sustain this phoneme for any extended period of time.)

EXERCISE 4.15

Hum the /m/ phoneme in an octave leap, opening the mouth for /ɑ/; retaining the same sense of resonance. Follow with a descent to the prime.

Exercise 4.15

Exercise 4.16

Begin directly on the fifth of the scale, in the region of the passage zone, with the phoneme /m/, changing to the vowel in descending to the prime. Follow it with the phoneme /n/ and the indicated subsequent vowel.

EXERCISE 4.17

Alternate the nasal phonemes /m/ and /n/, on the intervals of an octave and a fifth.

Exercise 4.17

EXERCISE 4.18.

In exercise 4.18, several cardinal vowels follow the nasal phoneme /n/mid-way in the phrase. Other nasals can be used in similar fashion.

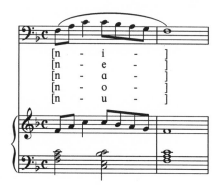

Exercise 4.18

Whereas it is clear that the three nasals /m/, /n/, and /ɲ/ connect portions of the entire resonator tube, the fourth nasal /ŋ/ entirely excludes the mouth as a resonator. The velum is in contact with the posterior portion of the tongue, a maneuver that cuts off mouth resonance. Resonating chambers of /ŋ/ consist of the nasal cavity, the pharynx, and the larynx. With the phoneme /ŋ/, the position of the mouth has minimal influence on the resulting sound. The mouth and lips may be in either a lateral or a rounded position. However, utmost care must be exercised to immediately remove any lingering nasality in the subsequent vowel.

EXERCISE 4.19

Exercise 4.19 couples the fourth nasal /ŋ/ with vowel sounds.

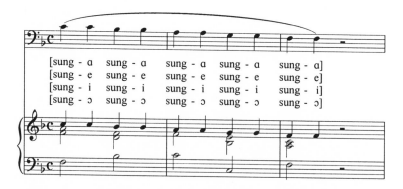

Exercise 4.19

An ancient check against nasality during all vowel production is to occlude the nostrils with finger and thumb at the precise moment the vowel makes its appearance. This is particularly the case following the presence of the nasal continuant /ŋ/. With the emergence of the vowel, there must be no emission of tone through the nose; there is a sudden cessation of nasality.

Chapter 5

VOWEL MODIFICATION ("COVER"), ENERGIZATION, AND RANGE EQUALIZATION

As soon as the baritone, bass-baritone, or bass concentrates on equalizing timbre from lower to middle and upper ranges, two important factors come to the fore: (1) a gradated increase in breath energy (but not a *higher* rate of breath expulsion), and (2) an adjustment of the vocal tract through vowel modification. Although we have looked at both of these areas in passing, we now concentrate on them from a somewhat different perspective. Our first consideration concerns the role breath energy—breath "support"—plays during the process of vowel modification and in timbre equalization.

As mentioned earlier, voice treatises have described the lower registration point as the "first register break," known historically as the primo passaggio. It also has been termed "the first lift of the breath," with the secondo passaggio then being called "the second register break" or "the second lift of the breath" (see chapter 1). Some teachers speak of "flipping over" at the second passaggio; others (God forgive!) refer to placing a "lid" on the tone, or to "hooking in" the voice. These descriptive phrases attempt to subjectively describe what is a learnable process, in accordance with natural vowel modification and breath-management adjustments. Systems that ask the singer to manufacture drastic mechanical changes in order to "cover" are excessive.

Building an even, stable scale is primary to the art of singing. It is best explained not as a mechanistic event but as the modification of sound that occurs during pitch ascent. As has been repeatedly pointed out thus far in this discussion, when in the speech-inflection range (modal or "chest"), the dictum "si canta come si parla" ought to pertain. As one raises the pitch beyond the range of the speaking voice, the mouth gradually opens, which increases the strength of the harmonic partials found in the lower portion of the spectrum, thus avoiding an exaggerated concentration of acoustic strength in the upper region of the spectrum. To retain the same relatively lateral mouth posture appropriate to the speech range, while raising the pitch of the singing voice to upper-range tessituras, can only result in overly bright, thin, shrill timbre. Therefore, in upper range one no longer sings with the same buccal aperture as pertained in the speech-inflection range. Drastically altering the resonance spectra is detrimental to vowel integrity and to the chiaroscuro balance. A gradual process is the answer.

The mouth gradually opens (that is, the jaw slightly lowers) as one goes from normal to forceful communication. I select a homey illustration to make the point. If the baritone has a close personal relationship with lovely young Jane, when he speaks intimately to her, saying "Jane," his mouth is in the lateral positions of the vowels [e] and [i] (or [ɪ]), spoken as a glide. If Jane walks away, he calls out "Jane!" at a higher pitch level, and his mouth opens slightly. If Jane has had it with him, and strides away in anger, he calls loudly "JANE!!" In so doing, his mouth opens yet farther. However, it does not assume the positions it would have if he to were to call out the names of "John," "Joan," or "June." (He wants only Jane to respond, not John, Joan, or June!) The point is that, even in heightened phonation, vowel integrity can be maintained. It can do so only if the vocal tract is permitted to maintain the proper balances among the resonators that allow for clean linguistic definition. This process is often termed "vowel-tracking."

"Covering" must serve to modify the vowel but ought not to destroy the integrity of the vowel. Where does the mouth begin the gradual process of additional opening? For the lyric baritone, that point generally corresponds to the B_3 pitch region (the primo passaggio, see chapter 1). However, the extent of the change in the vocal tract at that point in his scale is still minimal. A major problem for many lyric baritones is in opening the mouth excessively at the primo passaggio under the impression that it is necessary to do so to "cover" the tone. Then the production becomes too heavy for an easy ascent to the secondo passaggio that occurs around E_4 or $E\flat_4$.

The character of his instrument determines the extent to which a singer needs to "cover" at the secondo passaggio. Some baritones require a minimal degree of vowel modification at the pivotal registration notes, others a bit more. None need to make the dreaded "Ah-ooga!" sound of an old automobile horn for an intervallic leap from lower to upper voice. Ought every lyric baritone to modify the vowel exactly at the same note in the scale as do certain other baritones? Will all dramatic baritones modify at a given pitch? Will the bass-baritone and the bass conform rigidly to comparable specific "cover" points in the scale? The answer to all of those queries is a resounding "No!" Vowel modification is one of the most individualistic maneuvers of the male elite singing voice. The more dramatic baritone will undergo a gradual modification process beginning around B♭$_3$, the bass-baritone at A$_3$, and the bass at A♭$_3$ or at G$_3$. A more marked modification will take place roughly at the secondo passaggio, approximately at the interval of a fourth higher respectively for each fach. Yet, no universal rule is applicable.

My own preference, which I firmly believe to be in keeping with historic international pedagogy, is that natural modification of the vowel—together with an increase in breath energy—automatically assists in "covering" the phonation. There is no need for drastic alteration at the level of the pharynx or the larynx. Modifying results from natural acoustic accommodation. In proper modification, the larynx and the pharynx synergistically cooperate; the vocal tract responds in comfortable fine-tuning without distortion.

The expression "cover" is found in every major national school of singing: *copertura* in Italian; *couverture* in French; *Deckung* in German; *cover* in English. There is even some physical reality about the expression "to cover," in that the epiglottis, in response to movement of the tongue as the vowel-spectrum progresses from /i/ to /u/, more completely obscures the visibility of the vocal folds on the back vowels. This can be witnessed by fiber-optic examination. There is, incidentally, a wide divergence in the degree of epiglottic lowering from technique to technique, and from singer to singer.

The term "covering" is closely related to other frequently found expressions of international voice pedagogy: *voce aperta* and *voce chiusa*—literally "open voice" and "closed voice" (see chapter 16). These phenomena have solely to do with acoustic adjustments and do not refer to an open or a closed throat. "Open" phonation is the unmodified sound that results from raising the pitch without modifying the vowel. "Open singing" is described in several languages as *voce bianca, voix blanche, weisse Stimme,* and *white voice.*

There is an increase of breath energy as the baritone, bass-baritone, or bass leaves the speech-inflection range. (Please remember that increased energy does not denote a boost in volume nor in vocal effort.) It is impossible to separate acoustic aspects of the singing voice from breath-management events. The classic term "appoggio" refers to the coordination of breath pacing and resonance.

As a rule, in ascending pitch the front (lateral) vowels tend to require less adjustment because they already have about them the "chiusa" aspect of copertura. The back (rounded) vowels—being acoustically lower in upper partials than the front (lateral) vowels—may seem to require greater modification as the zona di passaggio is experienced.

Each individual instrument must discover the proper degree of copertura on lateral and rounded vowels. For every singer, the desire for an even, uninterrupted scale will determine at what point the vowel is to be modified, and the extent of that modification. In some respects, this is the most telling technical maneuver the low male voice must learn. Of course, ignoring the existence of register pivotal points makes the unified scale impossible.

A word of warning is in order. One of the most pressing problems in the teaching of singing comes from too great a concentration on the events of registration. A singer can become so focused on registration that the natural musical flow is interrupted. The even scale can only be established by complete awareness of the need for registration adjustments but without undue concentration devoted to its accomplishment. Gradual modification of the ascending vowel, and an increase in breath energy, produce the desirable even scale, the hallmark of the classical singing voice.

Chapter 6

MOVING INTO MIDDLE VOICE
(*ZONA DI PASSAGGIO*) AND ABOVE

Additional commentary on male registration is now in order. Perhaps the most crucial area of the male singing scale, historically designated as the zona di passaggio (the passage zone), lies between the speech range and the upper-mid range of the singing voice, an area also termed *voce media* (see chapter 1).

Ancient fragments of music from classic Greece and from Hebrew and Christian chant were restricted almost entirely to the speech-inflection region. As vocal boundaries expanded in response to cultural demands, singers began to sing in ranges beyond the speech span. Today's singing artist must command an impressive extension of the vocal scale. The inexperienced low-voiced singer tends to rely on "the call of the voice" to negotiate pitches that lie above the speech range, because that is what he does in normal life when he makes voiced sounds above the primo passaggio. He then depends on a quality termed "chest" or "modal." There are teachers of singing who advocate using this "call of the voice" beyond the regions of healthy function.

A widely differing approach, equally detrimental, is advocated in certain other quarters: the entire upper male range is based on falsetto quality (the imitative sound of the female voice in the male instrument). International historic voice pedagogy avoids both pitfalls through a gradual balancing of timbre as the vocal scale progresses upward. Sudden marked changes in quality are shunned.

The process of vowel modification begins at the point where ascending pitch encounters the zona di passaggio. Vowel modification enables the negotiation of pitches that lie above the passage zone. Several interchangeable international expressions well describe the vowel-modification process. One such term is *aggiustamento* (adjustment). As has been pointed out, registration is not an event that occurs suddenly for all vowels at an exact pivotal note that denotes the primo passaggio of the individual voice. Changes that occur within the voce media (zona di passaggio) require graduated adjustment. The term "aggiustamento" encompasses both breath-management factors and the acoustic events (resonance determinants) as the scale ascends.

Another international practical registration term is *arrotondamento*, which denotes the rounding of vowels so as to diminish shrill or open singing during the course of the mounting scale. A drawback to this term lies in its inherent implication that vowel modification must always be rounded toward a back vowel, whereas in the case of the vowels /u/ and /ʊ/, modification for the low male voice in its upper range may mean adjustment toward a more lateral vowel position. For these reasons, I rely chiefly on the expression "vowel modification." It envelops the widest number of possible exigencies.

Let us look at how best the zona di passaggio is integrated into the great scale (two octaves) of the singing voice.

Zona di passaggio Exercises for Lyric and Dramatic Baritone Voices

Begin with a brief pattern such as 1–3–4–3–1 in F major, with its origin in modal voice. Each cardinal vowel is consecutively treated. In the key of F, the exercise moves upward to touch the first note of the passage zone.

EXERCISES 6.1–6.4b

The singer progresses gradually through several ascending keys, introducing vowel and intervallic changes. Resonance sensations begin to alter as the voce media region is approached, but the aim is to maintain an equal balance among low and high formants. The singer must make certain that neither the "ring" nor the "depth" of the tonal quality alters. A uniformity of resonance prevails.

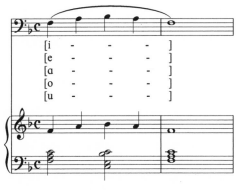

Exercise 6.1

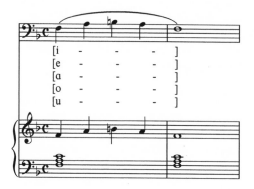

Exercise 6.2

Exercise 6.3a

Exercise 6.3b

Exercise 6.4a

Exercise 6.4b

Exercises for Baritone That Prepare for the Region of the *secondo passaggio*

EXERCISE 6.4C

Exercise 6.4c begins in lower-middle range and progresses through the zona di passaggio to the secondo passaggio pivotal point. As the secondo passaggio point is reached, the mouth begins to open more, and the vowel modifies in the direction of a neighboring vowel. Alternate a lateral and a rounded vowel.

Exercise 6.4c

EXERCISE 6.5

One of the most important of all registration exercises combines passaggi exercises into one grand entity, including major seventh, minor
seventh, and diminished seventh chords, as shown in exercise 6.5. In
the process, each note in the passage zone is approached from lower-
middle voice in a mounting, musical phrase. The aim is to smoothly
negotiate each interval as it relates to its neighboring interval. The
singer's ear must become attuned to uniformity.

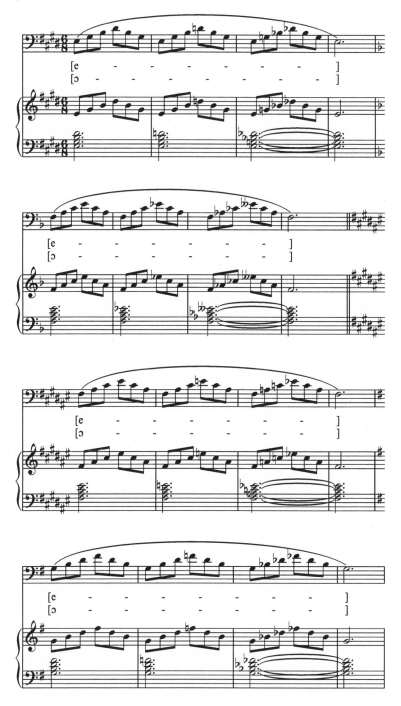

Exercise 6.5

In exercise 6.6a, the baritone combines enriched harmonic patterns beginning in the key of G major, moving through lower-middle-range pitches to those that lie above the secondo passaggio pivotal point.

Exercise 6.6a

Each phrase of exercise 6.6b progressively touches ascending and descending intervals in the zona di passaggio, requiring appropriate aggiustamento.

Exercise 6.6b

(continued)

Exercise 6.6b *(continued)*

EXERCISE 6.6C

Exercise 6.6c illustrates how in the key of E major, the bass-baritone and the bass may make use of the grand passaggio vocalise. Front and back vowels are alternately sung. Neighboring keys should be introduced.

Exercise 6.6c

All zona di passaggio exercises may be adjusted downward by a half to a whole tone for the bass-baritone, and by a minor third for the bass. Vowel modification happens at pitches properly geared to the passaggi events of each voice.

It is not possible to devise a universally applicable system to determine the exact extent to which all baritones, bass-baritones, and basses will modify a particular vowel. In the case of some lyric voices, lateral vowels will need to retain the high closure of the front vowel series; for example /ɛ/ will move closer to /e/. With other lyrics, the close front vowel will need to open toward a neighboring back vowel. For example /i/ will partake of the color of /ɪ/; the vowel /e/, the color of /ɛ/. In most instances of vowel modification, the back vowels will take on the shade of the next vowel in sequence. For example, /ɑ/ will be influenced by /ɔ/, /ɔ/ by /o/, /o/ by /ʊ/, and so on. The bass-baritone and the bass will, with rare exceptions, make earlier vowel modifications than will the lyric baritone. How can one tell how to proceed? By listening carefully for "seamlessness" in passing from one note to the other in the passage zone.

These exercises prove efficacious in the equalization of timbre within, and above, the zona di passaggio segments of the scale. It is not expected that a singer will tackle the whole series of passaggio exercises all at once but, rather, that he will gradually add more advanced maneuvers over a period of time, always in keeping with his individual rate of progress.

Because physical structure has so many possible variations—all of which determine the registration pivotal points in a voice—the trained musicianly ear is the only safe arbiter for determining the exact degree of vowel modification required for the phonetic shading of each vowel as it enters the passage zone.

Useful Passages from the Literature

The established, performing artist-singer will find his most worthwhile technical calisthenics within the standard literature. Pivotal register points and the demands of upper-range tessitura determine both breath management and resonance factors.

Excerpts should include contrasting technical tasks. Choice should be made of any aria phrase that includes thorny and climactic phrases or that demands high levels of finesse and stamina. After a singer establishes security on isolated climactic phrases, he gradually works backward from them, each time adding a few more phrases.

Passages from the repertoire should be included in every daily protocol. The following excerpts are chosen because they represent vocal and interpretive climaxes from noted sources. Climaxes in arias for baritones, bass-baritones, and basses generally occur in tessituras where aggiustamento is necessary. Clearly, the items a singer chooses should be undertaken only after good breath management, vowel differentiation, registration, vowel modification, sostenuto, and agility have been mastered, and after stamina has been established. (It would be vocal suicide for the inexperienced baritone, bass-baritone, or bass to embark on these demanding aria segments.)

It is well to hold in mind the old rubric, "practice makes permanent, not perfect." With that caveat in mind, we turn to some essential passages from the literature, sampled from several languages. Characteristic dramatic passages serve as registration-mapping fragments. I am not implying that composers consciously write vocalises for singers but, rather, that an experienced composer of music for the singing voice understands which vowels will produce the most favorable sounds at registration points.

English-Language Sources

Tabor's aria, "Warm as the Autumn Light," from *The Ballad of Baby Doe*, by Douglas Moore, from which literature example 6.1 is excerpted, couples an Americana flavor with Italianate bel canto phrasing. It is ideal for the emerging professional (not for the beginner). Cumulative phrases provide an excellent vehicle for breath renewal and sustained legato; the aria is a perfect study in vowel modification.

In the latter part of the fifth measure of the excerpt—on the name "Baby Doe"—Moore has built a classic zona di passaggio exercise for the baritone or bass-baritone. For most singers, the front vowels /e/ and /i/ of "Baby" begin slightly to modify toward /ɛ/ and /ɪ/. The vowels (/o/ and /u/), which share the sung syllable of "Doe," may move toward the more open vowels /ɔ/ and /ʊ/. However, with heavier instruments, the modification will tend toward

Literature Example 6.1

greater closure. In short, some singers will require little modification, others considerably more. Only the practiced ear can determine the right solution.

Bob's aria, "When the Air," from *The Old Maid and the Thief,* by Gian Carlo Menotti, from which literature example 6.2 is selected, is another English-language aria that recalls the bel canto style, transplanted by the composer from his native Italy to America. The dramatic cry "Ah!" /ɑ/ at F_4 must be vibrant, direct, and clean.

If the singer has tension problems in achieving a free, clean onset on the F_4, he should turn to the pilot device of a quick, introductory agility pattern on approaching pitches (1–2–3), or a rapid octave arpeggio (1–3–5–8). Inserting an agility pattern just prior to the onset is a general freedom-inducing tactic. Then drop the inserted agility pattern and reonset directly on the F_4 (see chapter 7).

Literature Example 6.2

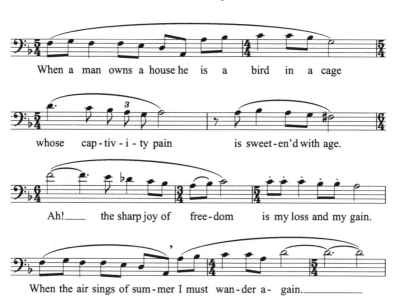

When a man owns a house he is a bird in a cage

whose cap-tiv-i-ty pain is sweet-en'd with age.

Ah!___ the sharp joy of free-dom is my loss and my gain.

When the air sings of sum-mer I must wan-der a-gain._____

Although notated in the treble clef, *Songs and Proverbs of William Blake,* from which literature example 6.3 is taken, was dedicated by Benjamin Britten to baritone Dietrich Fischer-Dieskau. The phrase "In ev'ry infant's cry of fear" quickly moves into the voce media (B♭–E♭$_4$). It progresses through a minor third above the secondo passaggio on "cry," playing with G♭$_4$ and F$_4$. Britten, who understood the intricacies of the singing voice in the zona di passaggio, juxtaposed several front vowels ("in ev'ry") on the pitches B♭$_3$, C$_4$, D$_4$, which lead to the sustained vowel /a/ ("ban") on the pivotal E♭$_4$. In all probability, the front vowels will open slightly in the ascending passage, and the word "ban" will modify from /a/ to /ɑ/, or in some voices, change even to the color of /ɔ/; the mouth slightly opens and rounds.

Literature Example 6.3

In ev - 'ry In - fant's cry of fear,

In ev - 'ry voice, in ev - 'ry ban,

The mind - forg'd ma - na - cles I hear.

Italian-Language Sources

The following arias are vocally and emotionally demanding. They play a major role in securing the professionally oriented voice.

"Largo al factotum" (*Il barbiere di Siviglia*, Gioachino Rossini), source of literature example 6.4, is considered by most professional baritones as the ultimate exemplar of high-lying flexibility. Much of the aria lodges in the passage zone and above. The singer must preserve a delicate balance between energy and relaxation, particularly in the rapid parlando passages. The triplet figures in the 6/8 patterns call for clean and vibrant execution.

Some baritones take the traditional liberty of resting out for a bar and a half before the penultimate "della città" to have fresh impetus for the four syllables of the final "della città!" In any event, a fermata of long duration is expected on the G4 of the syllable "ci-." The vowel must retain its lateral /i/ integrity, but the jaw lowers to increase mouth resonance. The zygomatic area

Literature Example 6.4

So - no il fac - to - tum del - la cit - tà,

so - no il fac - to - tum del - la cit - tà, del -

-la cit - tà, del - la cit - tà, del - la cit - tà!

should remain elevated. (For a splendid voice lesson, watch the old *Firestone Hour* video performance of Leonard Warren singing this aria!)

Puccini's *Edgar* is not part of the standard opera literature, but it includes several arias of much merit, among them "Questo amor." Once again we have an ideal study (literature example 6.5) in baritone registration practices. The close-intervallic treatment of phrases such as 'E lei sola, io sogno, bramo!' (measures 6–8 of the excerpt) invites an intensity of legato to be delivered in a quasi-portamento fashion. The final "Ah sventura!" (measure 11 of the excerpt) may be terminated on F_4 with an effective operatic release, followed by a dramatic onset on the subsequent "L'amo!" or it can be carried onward through the next "L'amo!" with no loss of intensity. "Questo amor" is distinguished by surging romanticism. It provides a brief but passionate exposition that gives competition adjudicators a chance to assess the singer's competency in the romantic, verismo style.

Germont's aria from *La traviata* (Verdi), from which literature examples 6.6a and 6.6b have been chosen, is one of the most beloved items in the baritone opera repertoire. Much of the aria lies in the passage zone with sustained climactic phrases in upper voice. "Di Provenza il mar, il suol" is a study in the juxtaposition of emotive semistaccato and legato singing, with a near-portamento intensity in the legato segments. It has great value as an exercise for ironing out the zona di passaggio and the notes immediately lying above the passage zone. The aria demonstrates warmth and persuasiveness, subtly combined in a single vocal and dramatic manifestation. It is not simply a display vehicle—although admittedly among the foremost of arias on that account alone—but an expression that requires deep psychological penetra-

Oh ram-men-ta pur nel duol ch'i-vi gio-ia_a te bril-lò, e che

pa - ce co - là sol su te splen-de-re_an-cor può, e che

pa - ce co - là sol su te splen-de-re_an-cor può.

Dio mi gui-dò, Dio mi gui-dò! Dio mi gui-dò!

tion. The aria's sentiment reveals the true character of Germont as he attempts to control the lives of Alfredo and Violetta. It is the solo companion piece to his magnificent duet with Violetta, which reveals his cunning method of persuasion.

As a practice plan, execute the whole excerpted segment of example 6.6a on a front vowel such as /e/, then on a back vowel as with /ɔ/, and subsequently on the mixed vowel /œ/. Return to the inherent vowels of the text (consonants still omitted), sung in legato mode. Finally, the original text is added, with the consonants crisply articulated. The three phrases set to the text "Dio mi guidò" are tailor-made for baritone vowel modification and for resonance balancing. This excerpt may be broken down into shorter, separate phrases.

The repeated "Dio mi guidò" places the vowels /i/ and /ɔ/ in adjacent positions; this juxtaposition makes an exemplary study in the balancing of resonance as the singer progresses from front to back vowels in high range. Vowel integrity must be maintained, but the timbre has to be equalized by the application of the aggiustamento process. A smooth, uniform quality of sound is dependent on the efficient "rounding" adjustment of the resonator tract.

The second statement of the phrase "e che pace colà sol su te splendere ancor può" is another superlative study in vowel differentiation and modification. The same practice devices suggested for earlier segments of the aria could be fruitfully applied here.

The second strophe of "Di Provenza" (example 6.6b), from the phrase "se la voce dell'onor," onward through the final "Dio m'esaudì!" offers a particular challenge with its repeated G♭$_4$ onset on the syllable "ma" at the cadenza phrase "ma . . . ma se alfin ti trovo ancor," which concludes with the final "Dio m'esaudì!" The dramatic fermata and the subsequent pause should be given full value so that the first 'ma' onset at G♭$_4$ can be somewhat delayed. The release of the sound should be as precise and clean as its onset; there must be a distinctive operatic release. A marked pause is necessary between the two "ma" onsets on G♭$_4$. Although some established singers omit the re-onset on G♭$_4$ at "ma," it ought to be included to achieve the full emotional impact of the concluding passages of the aria, and because it definitively shows the singer's technical prowess in attacking, releasing, and reonsetting at full voice on pitches in high range. Axial body alignment and the complete appoggio are indispensable to this aria.

As a practice tool, in approaching each G♭$_4$ insert a brief vibrant pilot phrase composed of rapid sixteenth notes in a 1–2–3–4 pattern in advance of

Literature Example 6.6b

the target note. Then drop the steering notes and return to the direct onset as written. Another device is to momentarily insert a rapid seventh-chord arpeggio, which rockets upward from middle voice to Gb_4. Execute the insertion a number of times, then discontinue the supplemental inducement strategies and sing the phrase as Verdi intended.

In the performance of these excerpted Verdi segments, it must be kept in mind that the aim is a middle road between too much "cover" and too much "voce aperta." By the time the crucial high note is reached, the production may tend to become overweighted. The answer is not the usual "just keep it high and light" admonition of the forward-placement pedagogue, but an understanding of the gradation process of vowel modification. There is not a set vowel position throughout the passage; there is gradual resonator tract alteration that comes from lip rounding, zygomatic-arch elevation, jaw relaxation, and an increase in the appoggio factor. The even scale results.

In numerous instances, Verdi's demands on the baritone go well beyond the requirements of earlier composers. As previously mentioned (see chapter 1), conductors and artistic directors identify a "Verdi baritone" as a sturdy baritone voice that can maintain a high tessitura and project emotional intensity. An ultimate study of passaggio events for the established Verdi baritone is found in the aria "Il balen del suo sorriso" (*Il trovatore*), with its upper-range tessitura and its call for flexibility in cumulative phrases. Yet another exemplar is Iago's "Credo in un Dio" (*Otello*) with its high tessitura and dramatic $F\sharp_4$s. Only the most mature, secure baritone should attempt either aria. (Because of space considerations excerpts from these extremely demanding dramatic arias have not been included.)

The Leoncavallo *Pagliacci* opening aria "Si può? Si può?" requires a mature, rangy baritone voice capable of both lyricism and dramatic stamina. The aria combines quasi recitativo sections, arioso vocal excursions, and long segments of sustained high-lying phrases in a grand display of theatrical writing. Its opportunities for intimate communication and exhibition vocalism are unlimited. The phrase "e che di quest'orfano mondo al pari di *voi* spiriamo l'aere!" with a leap to the universally interpolated Ab_4 on the syllable

Literature Example 6.7

MOVING INTO MIDDLE VOICE (*ZONA DI PASSAGGIO*) AND ABOVE   75 "voi," is a valuable extract for the established baritone who is technically and emotionally ready to take on this substantial hurdle. (If the A♭$_4$ is not performed, the baritone will probably have presented the aria in vain.)

As mentioned, a clever practice-room plan is to approach sustained high pitches by prefacing each with a rapid arpeggio, or through a vital short 1–2–3 or 1–2–3–4 agility pattern.

"Voi" must undergo modification tailored to the individual voice. The exact form of aggiustamento for one singer may be the opening of the initial vowel toward the phoneme /ɔ/. For someone else, the vowel may best be modified by taking the direction of /œ/. Still another baritone will need to shade toward /ʊ/ or /u/. "Cover" cannot be achieved by adhering to an immutable aggiustamento rule where one size, and one space, fits all.

With the modification of the vowel, the singer must ensure optimal "noble" axial compactness of the head/neck/shoulder complex, and external muscular frame-support of the larynx. There will be a significant increase in appoggio expansion. These physical features are fused into one Gestalt. Psychologically, the singer should experience the excitation and the elation present in all heightened physical activity.

The traditional G$_4$ interpolation on the syllable "cia" of the word "Incominc*iate*!" (an electrifying final climax) is essential. The *ossia* indications (alternate versions) have become part of accepted tradition. In practice sessions, the G$_4$ should be prepared by means similar to those used in approaching the A♭$_4$ on "voi" (see earlier). The baritone prefaces the note with brief agility patterns, as in exercise 6.7 and exercise 6.8. He then drops the inserted notes and returns to the original version.

EXERCISES 6.7 AND 6.8

cia - - - te

Exercise 6.7

cia - - - te

Exercise 6.8

Following a lengthy exposition of sustained singing that hovers in the zona di passaggio, Leoncavallo has set up a perfect approach to the final climax. Did he anticipate the traditional interpolation of the G$_4$? In any event, he provides a quasi-recitative interlude before the concluding phrase. Each baritone must discover the exact degree of modification necessary to keep the chiaroscuro balance present throughout sustained high phrases. Although vowel integrity and good diction ought to be maintained, when it comes to stratospheric pitches, timbre takes precedence over enunciation.

As a practice device, any high-lying phrase may first be doubled in tempo; then the tempo intended by the composer is reestablished.

French-Language Sources

Practically every phrase of the recitative "O sainte médaille" and of the aria "Avant de quitter ces lieux" (*Faust*, Gounod) offers a study in registration equalization. Phrase shapes of the aria exemplify how excerpts from the literature provide roadmaps for handling technical issues. (Examples are for the advanced singer.)

"Délivré d'une triste pensée," from the più animato section of the aria through "j'irai combattre pour mon pays," offers an excellent juxtaposition of front and back vowels within the zona di passaggio, and above. The phrase "Délivré" leads to F_4 on the front vowel /e/ ("pensée"), and courses through the passage zone at a moderately rapid tempo. It serves as a fine model for vowel modification in an agility setting. The close French /e/ of "pensée" should remain a fully frontal vowel, despite the need to modify it to avoid excessive concentration of acoustic strength in the area of the singer's formant (roughly 2800Hz–3000Hz). Vowel integrity must be retained. The jaw opens

Literature Example 6.8

to accommodate high pitch and to modify the vowel. Vowels /i/ of "ennem*is*" and /ɑ/ of "br*a*ve" (respectively at E♭$_4$ and G♭$_4$) must show evidence of true chiaroscuro balance. In order to do so, both vowels undergo a process of neutralization, assured by opening the mouth more fully. Similarly the /e/ of "mêl*é*e" and the vowel /ɑ/ of "comb*a*ttre" proffer a superb study in the equalization of front and back vowel configurations. Furthermore, the middle syllable of "comb*a*ttre" makes a splendid exercise in zona di passaggio treatment. Its triplet-turn on E♭$_4$, D$_4$, F$_4$, E♭$_4$, C$_4$, A♭$_3$, and its conclusion in lower-middle voice at C$_4$, B♭$_3$, G$_3$, E♭$_3$, A♭$_3$ (more than an octave), is as fine a passaggio exercise as has ever been devised. "Comb*a*ttre" hovers around the upper pivotal registration point at the precise location where vowel modification and voce chiusa must conjoin. (The aria was originally written in English for a specific baritone for an English-language production during Gounod's London stay. During Gounod's lifetime, the published score of *Faust* did not include the aria. Despite its interesting initial history, the aria remains a foremost study of vowel modification in the French language.)

Although the dictionary shows the final syllable (tre) of a word such as "combattre" as a vanishing vowel, in singing, the schwa /ə/ must preserve the harmonic balance of the mixed vowel /œ/. Neutralizing it will deprive it of its necessary "ring."

The climactic passage from the Valentin aria—"ma soeur je confie! Ô roi des cieux, jette les yeux"—offers a prime example of the principle of vowel modification (literature example 6.9).

"Avant de quitter ces lieux" must be performed in the original key of E♭, not in the D♭ transposition in which it appears in some opera anthologies. A singer who presents the aria in D♭ at competitions or for auditions may be undermining his chances of placing. (Transposition decisions during performance lie in the hands of the conductor; an adjudication panel will insist on the original key.)

A high-lying sequence begins at E♭$_4$, on the vowel /ɑ/, the first vowel of the back vowel series. (In some phonetic systems, the vowel /ɑ/ is considered a part of the neutral or central vowel sequence.) The passage proceeds through

Literature Example 6.9

F_4, G_4, $B\flat_3$, $A\flat_3$, G_3, $A\flat_3$, G_3, and F_3. It begins exactly at the secondo passaggio of most operatic baritones. As pointed out earlier, the mouth opens at high-lying passages but the zygomatic muscles remain mildly elevated. If the baritone finds difficulty in accomplishing the proper modification on the vowel /ɑ/, he should first sing the entire passage on the mixed vowel /œ/. By its very structure, the mixed vowel /œ/ augments the upper partials associated with the singer's formant, while retaining the strength of the first formant. Proceed from the mixed vowel /œ/ to the back vowel /ɔ/, keeping the same "ring" and "depth" in the timbre. Then return to the vowels as they appear in the text. Finally, add the consonants, enunciating clearly.

For the Bass-Baritone and for the Bass

Italian-Language Sources

Each of the segments here quoted is the kind of literature source a bass-baritone should sing daily to secure the passage zone. The same rules of "cover" (vowel modification) presented earlier for baritone voices pertain to lower voice categories as well. It must be kept in mind that registration events occur a half tone lower for the bass-baritone, and a whole tone lower for the bass than they do for the baritone.

With the role of Leporello, in *Don Giovanni*, Mozart established one of the most gratifying stage concepts ever envisioned for the bass-baritone. Leporello set future expectations for the operatic bass-baritone and bass voice categories. Psychological ramifications and opportunities for elite vocalism are unbounded. Within "Madamina! Il catalogo è questo," Mozart presents the bass-baritone or bass a guide for registration equalization. Nearly every phrase in the aria serves as a passaggio vocalise. Because it is such a classic reservoir of registration events, a number of phrases from the aria will be treated in some detail.

For many bass-baritones and for some lyric basses, A_3 is the primo passaggio pivotal note, with D_4 the pivotal secondo passaggio registration point. The passage zone lies between A_3 and D_4. In literature example 6.10 ("Cento in Francia, in Turchia novant'una, Ma in Ispagna son già mille e tre!"), a re-iterated A_3 progresses to secondo passaggio D_4 on "Ma." It offers a fine introductory registration passage for the bass-baritone, The danger lies in sudden "covering" at the isolated passaggio note, or, conversely, of a lack of modification (voce bianca).

The rapid zona di passaggio parlando of "V'han contesse, baronesse" (literature example 6.11) requires fully vibrant singing, never straight-tone pattering. The phrase "d'ogni forma, d'ogni età!" plays with back and front vow-

Cen-to in Fran-cia, in Tur-chia no-van-t'u-na; Ma in I-

spa-gna, ma in I - spa-gna son già mil-le e tre!

els. The excerpt extends through E_4, on rapidly executed front vowels and on the sustained /o/ at "d'*o*gni." E_4 clearly lies above the secondo passaggio of most bass-baritones or basses. As with the baritone's handling of pitches comparable for his fach, there is no universal modification that suits every bass-baritone or bass voice. In some cases, the vowel opens toward /ɔ/; in others, the singer approaches the more pronounced back vowel /ʊ/. Another route may be to turn to the mixed vowel /œ/. Optionally, move from /œ/ through /ɔ/ to the more rounded /o/, /ʊ/, or /u/.

Literature Example 6.11

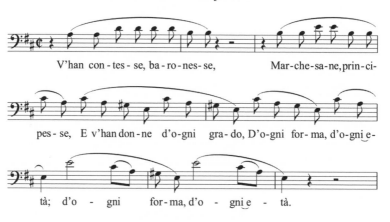

V'han con - tes - se, ba - ro - nes - se,   Mar-che-sa-ne, prin-ci-

pes - se, E v'han don-ne d'o-gni   gra-do, D'o-gni for-ma, d'o-gni e-

tà;   d'o - gni   for-ma, d'o - gni e - tà.

Literature Example 6.12

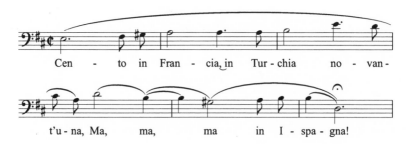

Cen - to in Fran - cia, in Tur - chia no - van-

t'u - na, Ma,   ma,   ma   in I - spa - gna!

The passage "Cento in Francia, in Turchia novant'una, Ma, ma, ma in Ispagna" (literature example 6.12) rises to E_4 at "*no*vant'una," which note requires considerable modification. Descending pitches on the subsequent "Ma, ma, ma" segment make an excellent study in both voce media equalization and onset accuracy.

Literature example 6.13 repeats "d'ogni forma, d'ogni età" in yet other arduous measures that often tax even the most accomplished singer. Some practical devices may assist: (1) sing the inherent vowels (an /o–i–ɔ–ɑ–o–i–e–ɑ/ sequence) without the consonants; (2) substitute a single vowel for the entire passage; (3) augment the tempo to double time; and (4) incorporate brief pilot agility passages before the onsets. Return to the phrases as written. Try the passage at a quick tempo until the vowel modification seems appropriate, then return to the original tempo. Once again, substitute the vowel sequence /o–i–ɔ–ɑ–o–i–e–ɑ/. Using the hand mirror, check the shapes of mouth and lips to be certain they conform to the vowel changes.

Literature Example 6.13

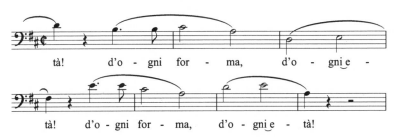

Coming where it falls within the aria, "E la grande maestosa" (and its repetition) may prove demanding for bass-baritones and lyric basses. Mozart has generously inserted a quarter rest at several points. A useful temporary practice-room device is to substitute onset notes for the quarter rests (third beat) of the 3/4 measures; that is, instead of observing the rest, insert a detached onset. At each onset insertion, breath renewal is immediate—the vocal folds fully part, which means total respite. Soon the inserted syllable is removed. Subsequently, in singing the phrase as written, breath renewal is accomplished in the same fashion: silently, and completely.

Literature Example 6.14

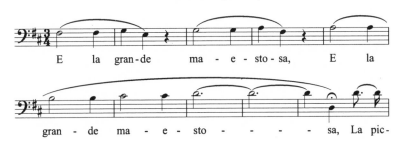

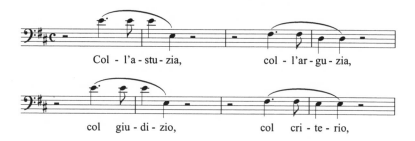

"La vendetta," Bartolo's classic rage aria, comes from Mozart's *Le nozze di Figaro*. The aria hovers around D_4 and E_4. Sudden onsets occur on E_4, at "Coll' astuzia," "coll' arguzia," and "col criterio." Mozart wisely gives the singer a preparatory pause before each demanding E_4 onset. The jaw and mouth will be properly opened, but the zygomatic muscles ought not to be pulled downward, and the chiaroscuro tone with its balance of "ring" and "depth" must remain in evidence (literature example 6.15). Mozart clearly had bass passaggio coloration in mind. He begins the phrases above the singer's secondo passaggio.

In literature example 6.16 ("conosce Bartolo"), Mozart approaches the pivotal registration point D_4 (excerpt measure 6) through the leap of an octave (D_3–D_4) and later by intervals of a fourth (A_3–D_4). A practice device is to insert a rapid pilot arpeggio (made up of D_3, $F\sharp_3$, A_4, D_4); it also may prove useful in preparatory study to add the passing notes in a rapid gruppetto (see chapter 7) between the intervallic leaps of the fourth, as a temporary approach to the octave D_3–D_4 leap.

Literature Example 6.16

"La calunnia" from Rossini's *Il barbiere di Siviglia* is a major repertoire challenge for the low-voiced male. Because of its high-lying tessitura, tradition permits transposition of the aria downward by half a tone for the bass-baritone. When a basso is cast as Don Basilio, the aria on occasion has been transposed to the key of C major. It is presented here in its original tonality.

Following the aria's beginning, brief legato passages are interrupted by series of onsets that provide a comparison of vocal sostenuto and detached onset activities. Each syllable of "in-co-min-cia, in-co-min-cia a su-sur-rar" should be vibrant with a distinct beginning and an exact termination. It is a classic onset vocalise, reminiscent of the "Ha-ha-ha-ha-Ha!" onsets that should remain a part of the daily regimen.

Literature Example 6.17

In literature example 6.18 "vola già di loco in loco, sembra il tuono, la tempesta che nel sen della foresta va fischiando, brontolando, e ti fa d'orror gelar. Alla fin trabocca e scoppia, si propaga, si raddoppia e produce un' esplosione," there is constant play between A_3–D_4, and D_4–E_4, as though Rossini were giving a voice lesson in traversing from the voce media (A_3–D_4) to the secondo passaggio pivotal note for bass voice and to the first note in the register that lies above the zona di passaggio. Although in patter mode, every note must retain a full-bodied, vibrant timbre and dare not fall prey to a light parlando.

vo - la già di lo-co in lo - co, sem-bra il tuo - no, la tem-

pe - sta che nel sen del - la fo - re - sta va fi-schian- do, bron-to -

lan- do, e ti fa d'or-ror ge - lar. Al - la fin tra-boc - ca e

scop- pia, si pro-pa - ga, si rad-dop-pia e pro-du - ce un'e-splo - sio-ne

co-me un col-po di can - no - ne, co-me un col-po di can - no -

ne, un tre-muo-to, un tem-po - ra - le, un tre-muo-to, un tem-po -

ra - le, un tre-muo-to, un tem-po - ra - le che fa l'a - ria rim-bom-

bar, un tre-muo-to, un tem-po - ra - le, un tre-muo-to, un tem-po -

ra - le, un tre-muo-to, un tem-po - ra-le che fa l'a - ria rim-bom- bar!

Rossini, as he often does at climaxes, gives the singer a moment's respite before the demanding "come un colpo di cannone" segment with its sustained Eb_4 and E_4 pitches that call for both vocal litheness and massive sound. The "no" syllable of the word "can*no*ne" is sustained on the first note (Eb_4) beyond the secondo passaggio pivotal point (D_4). The singer repeats the syllabic pattern on Eb_4, before moving to the sustained "no" at the reiterated "can*no*ne" on natural E_4, which lies above the secondo passaggio pivotal point.

Literature Example 6.19

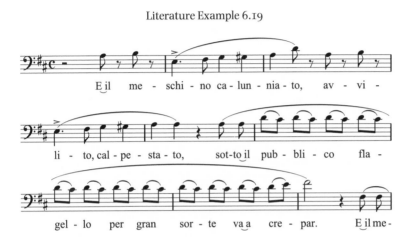

E il me - schi - no ca - lun - nia - to,   av - vi -

li - to, cal - pe - sta - to,   sot-to il pub - bli - co   fla -

gel - lo   per   gran   sor - te   va a   cre - par.   E il me -

The vowel on the second syllable of the "cre*par*" at $F\#_4$ (literature example 6.19) will probably need to be modified toward /u/ or even to /ʊ/. Another solution may be to modify /ɑ/ in the direction of /ø/. These suggestions, which at first glance may seem excessive, are appropriate because the pitch $F\#_4$ comes near the highest-lying publicly performable pitch in many low voices, and because the weightier the instrument, the more extensive the vowel modification needed. The reiterated duples on D_4–$C\#_4$ have to remain vibrant in order to approach the fully supported climactic $F\#_4$.

That these pitches play repeatedly with the second passaggio event (the $C\#_4$–D_4) running onward to a sostenuto at the syllable "par" of "cre*par*" would not have been unintentional by a composer who so well understood the constraints of the elite singing voices with which he regularly dealt. In this excerpt, Rossini gives the low-voiced male singer a splendid lesson in passaggio training.

Chapter 7

THE AGILITY FACTOR

Although I have made oblique reference to the usefulness of agility, this important aspect of technical mastery has not yet been fully considered. Many of the exercises and the musical excerpts encountered thus far were proposed to increase the singer's sustaining ability. Of equal importance is the capability to move the voice.

Sostenuto and agility are equivalent poles of the art of bel canto. A cavatina/cabaletta structure is characteristic of many nineteenth-century arias, for both male and female voices. This twofold compositional form contrasts sustained and melismatic bravura passages. Baritones, bass-baritones, and basses must have as great a facility to execute both fioriture (ornaments, embellishments, and cadenzas) and sostenuto passages as do the higher voices.

The agility factor grows directly out of the brief onset, to which it is closely related. Agility is present in laughter or panting (see chapter 2). I have already suggested that brief agility patterns can serve as liberating pilot approaches in high, sustained singing. It is time to consider agility in general.

EXERCISE 7.1

In developing velocity for elite singing, it is nonproductive to begin by practicing extended melismas (runs). The best procedure is to start with a few short, rapid figures in staccato mode that terminate on a sustained note. Lateral and rounded vowels should be alternated. Each of the brief phrases, whether staccato or legato, is to be sung with a continuous degree of energy until the moment of release. The precise release becomes the new breath.

Exercise 7.1

EXERCISE 7.2

Follow the staccato mode by singing the same pattern legato, being certain that the release of the note on the fermata incorporates the new silent breath.

Exercise 7.2

EXERCISE 7.3

Juxtapose the two modes (staccato and legato) within a single exercise. The same articulatory motions in the abdominal wall pertain for both staccato and legato modes.

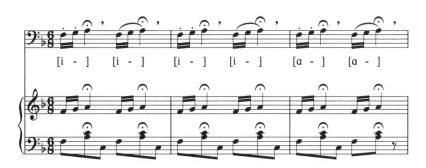

Exercise 7.3

EXERCISE 7.4

Extend the melismatic process to include gruppetti made up of six-teenth notes in slightly longer phrases. Each note must be fully vi-brant and well articulated. Make certain that the release becomes the new, silent breath. Begin in low range and gradually move upward by semitones through four or five keys. Listen for accurate pitch center-ing, particular in the descending gesture. It goes without saying that each note must be fully vibrant. At all costs, avoid any intrusion of straight tone.

Exercise 7.4

EXERCISE 7.5A

Exercise 7.5a combines the gruppetti into a longer sequence on /i–e–ɑ–e–i/. Move the indicated pattern upward by half tones until the zona di passaggio region is involved.

Exercise 7.5a

EXERCISE 7.5B

Exercise 7.5b initiates the vowel sequence /ɔ–e–i–e–ɔ/ on the same pattern as in exercise 7.5a.

Exercise 7.5b

As was previously pointed out, an awareness of articulatory sensation should be perceived in the abdominal region, but there is neither inward pulling nor outward distention of the epigastric region or of the abdominal wall. The epigastrium and the abdomen retain their initial inspiratory postures throughout each brief exercise. As patterns are elongated, some slight increase in inward movement may be apparent in the epigastric region, but the ribs, and the muscle sheath that extends from the pelvis to the fifth rib, remain close to their inhalatory positions.

As patterns progress from lower to upper ranges, a readjustment of breath energy is demanded. The singer should alter intonation levels, dropping from upper range to middle or low range, then back again to higher range. In keys such as G, A♭, A, and B♭, the velocity vocalises become rapid vowel modification drills as well.

Agility Passages from the Literature for the Baritone

Although "Sì, tra i ceppi" from Handel's *Berenice* was written for a contralto castrato, it has become a standard part of the baritone repertory. The long melisma on "risplenderà!" is an excellent vehicle for inducing articulated legato-agility capability. It will help to give a slight accented impulse to the first note of each gruppetto. A young baritone may find it necessary to break this extended melisma, in which case he should take a breath following a half-note/quarter-note tie. An accomplished baritone will sail through the entire phrase length as indicated in literature example 7.1. The passage can be transposed into neighboring keys, to serve as a standard daily exercise.

No better melismatic vocalise has ever been written for the mature baritone than the climactic conclusion of the Mozart *Figaro* aria "Hai già vinta la causa." In literature example 7.2 I have indicated traditional phrasing and breath-renewal possibilities. In the eighth measure of the citation, a quick

breath renewal is suggested after the eighth-notes of "mi *fa*," which lead directly into the long melisma on the last syllable of "giu-bi-*lar*," much of it on triplets. If the singer has properly mastered the quick breath replenishment drilled on the onset exercises (see chapter 3), this will be a welcome suggestion.

As every baritone knows, the $F\sharp_4$, on the syllable "fa" (measure seventeen of the excerpt) is the "cash note" of the aria. The singer who remains agile

Literature Example 7.2

and free at the close of this strenuous aria displays vocal prowess. The Count does not express anger in the long melisma. It is not a "rage melisma" but the anticipation of joyous vindication. *Figaro* passages should become part of daily routining.

Literature Example 7.3

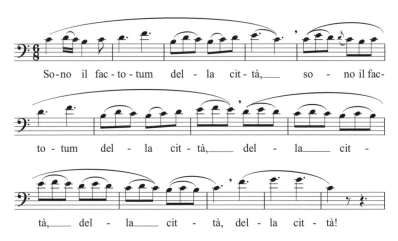

We encountered the Rossini example 7.3 in the vowel-modification discussion. The excerpt is also one of the most important agility passages in the repertoire. It is revisited here for the sake of convenience. Articulatory movement reminiscent of laughter or quiet panting, as earlier suggested, should be experienced in this segment. Lightness and completeness of timbre are achieved only within fully supported velocity. The triplet patterns must maintain voce completa quality.

Literature Example 7.4

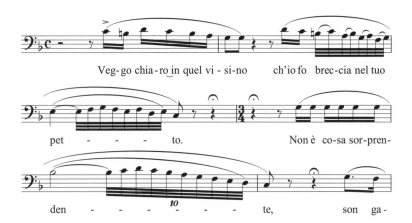

The aria "Come Paride vezzoso" from Donizetti's *L'elisir d'amore* has been chosen as a study in agility because it is suitable to low-voiced professionally oriented males at several levels of development. Although in performance a certain degree of rubato is appropriate, as an exercise the excerpted melismas should be practiced in strict rhythm. There must be no slurring of the extended velocity patterns on "*pet*-to," and "sor-pren-*den*-te." In the latter, the bass-baritone encounters the pivotal registration D_4 in a rapid passage that may offer insights as to its general modification. It may prove beneficial to practice it at both slow and quick tempos (literature example 7.4).

Literature Example 7.5

From the same source comes a somewhat more taxing agility passage, appropriate to either emerging or mature voices. The customary phrasing of "cede a Marte, Dio guerriero, fin la madre dell'Amor" is indicated in the excerpt. A breath renewal is traditionally taken. Linger over the upper notes as noted by the fermatas. Otherwise, the patterns should be executed with rhythmic accuracy (literature example 7.5).

For a change of pace in style and language, look at the final song, "Crab-bèd Age and Youth," from the Rorem cycle *From an Unknown Past.* It is of particular pedagogic value to the young baritone, because it plays agilely on the zona di passaggio, with C_4–E_4 reiterations, first on the vowel /ɛ/ of the syllable "plea-" of the word "pleasance," then on the vowel /e/ with the word "brave." It should be sung at varying tempi, eventually arriving at a very rapid rate of execution (literature example 7.6).

Agility Passages from the
Literature for the Bass-Baritone
and the Bass

Agility factors are as important to the bass-baritone and to the bass as to the baritone. Some of the excerpted examples earlier suggested for baritone are equally suited to the bass-baritone and to the bass. Another of much merit is the J. S. Bach *Weihnachtsoratorium* "Grosser Herr und starker König" (literature example 7.7).

The aria combines grandeur with vocal agility. The excerpt begins with the last sixteen bars before the instrumental interlude, and samples the rhythmic impulse characteristic of the entire aria, with strong dancelike offbeat accents. It proves a vigorous study in the juxtaposition of syllabic and melismatic interjections. "Grosser Herr" moves through the passage zone with dynamism. The aria demands vital expression and vibrant timbre. The extended melisma of the excerpted passage (on the word "Pracht") makes a first-rate agility exercise for the daily regimen. As a practice device, it can be profitably transposed up or down to near-neighbor keys.

The familiar low-voiced rage aria "Why do the nations so furiously rage" (literature example 7.8) from Handel's *Messiah*, evokes a genre with a long musicological history. The rage aria had already been firmly established in numerous early Italian operas and in Purcell's English-language works. The arpeg-

giated opening phrase, which extends over the range of a tenth, followed by a descending agility C-major scale, combines passaggio and agility exercises.

The triplet figure of measures 9 and 10 (literature example 7.8) outlines scalewise melodic progressions that lead to the climactic sustained D_4. As we have seen, for a number of bass-baritones and basses, D_4 is a crucial pivotal registration note. This passage illustrates the gradation of vowel migration in its arrival at the dramatic half-note D_4. A useful practice is to eliminate the triplet pattern for a moment, and to sing only the first note of each triplet gruppetto of measures 9 and 10 in the pitch series B–A–A–G–G–F♯–F♯–E–G–A–B–A–D. Then, at a reduced tempo, add the embellishing notes of the pattern. Gradually increase the tempo up to performance speed. If a single pitch of the series goes straight, the intensity of the phrase is lost. This powerful expression requires fullness of chiaroscuro timbre.

From the same aria (literature example 7.9) I have selected "Why do the people imagine a vain thing?" The quotation rhythmically varies the extended melisma through consecutive triplets, sixteenth-note/eighth-note segments, and a series of eighth-note duples. A superb vocalise is generated, proving again Handel as a great source for the elite singing voice. It cannot be too often repeated that, among composers, Handel and Mozart are foremost trainers of the singing voice.

Literature Example 7.8

Why do the na - tions so fu-rious-ly rage to - ge-ther? Why
do the peo-ple im - ag - ine a vain thing? Why do the na - tions
rage_____
__ so fu - rious - ly__ to - ge - ther?

Literature Example 7.9

why do the peo-ple im - a - - - -
- - - - - gine a vain thing, im -
- a - - - - - gine a vain thing?

With the majesty of "And I will shake the heavens, the earth, the sea and the dry land, and I will shake all nations," we arrive at one of the most telling of melismas conceived for male low voice. The first note of each sixteenth-note gruppetto must mark the melodic contour of the phrase, but every note of each gruppetto ought to display the same completeness of timbre—voce completa—that distinguishes the chiaroscuro principle (literature example 7.10).

Literature example 7.11 (Haydn's *The Creation*, "Rolling in Foaming Billows") presents melismatic movement that contrasts with the vigorous vocalism of the preceding Handel excerpts. Haydn's melismas flow languidly "through open plains outstretching wide." Its "serpent error" is unhurried, flowing moderately to the sustained D_4. Absent is the Handelian rage, which does not make the Haydn a more easily produced velocity pattern. The some-

what relaxed tempo, and the serpentine melodic direction taken by the musical figure may falsely invite a reduction of energy, which could cause the singer to fall into the fault of undersinging. The same rules of gradated vowel modification that pertain to swiftly moving "runs" must be operative here at the slower tempo.

Literature Example 7.11

Once again we turn to Rossini's "La calunnia," from *Il barbiere di Siviglia,* to find an admirable exercise in vocal agility. Pitches of the excerpt play re-

peatedly with the second passaggio event (the C♯4–D$_4$ event) running onward to a sostenuto at the syllable "par" of cre*par*. The duples must press forward. In this excerpt, Rossini gives the low-voiced singer a splendid lesson in passaggio as well as agility training (literature example 7.12).

The nineteenth-century device of the vocal half-staccato is skillfully employed at the repetition of the text "E il meschino calunniato, avvilito, calpestato, sotto il pubblico flagello." It produces a degree of vocal insistency that underscores the meaning of the words. To treat the passage in modern staccato fashion is to misunderstand its stylistic intent. Only the section "sotto il pubblico fla-" is to be broken, as though it were an exercise in onset and release.

Literature example 7.13 for the buffo bass begins at "A un dottor della mia sorte queste scuse, signorina!" (*Il barbiere di Siviglia,* Rossini). The quickly moving gruppetto onsets that occur very expressively in the first and second systems of the excerpt must be clean and vibrant; they are not to be tossed away in parlando fashion. The thirty-second-note descending melismas remain strongly pitch-centered, without slurring. Breath renewals ought never to interrupt the relentless forward rhythm. Interjectory short phrases beginning at "Via, carina, confessate!" need to carefully preserve the dotted rhythmic values.

Buffo bass roles are not simply dramatic diversions but serve as elite singing roles. They require the same levels of velocity skill as do roles of a se-

chiar.A un Dot-tor del-la mia sor-te que-ste scu-se, si-gno-

-ri-na! Vi con-si-glio, mia ca-ri-na, un po-co me-glio a im-po-stu-

rar, un____ po' me-glio a im-po-stu-

rar, un___ po'___ me-glio, un po'me-glio a im-po-stu-rar!

Via, ca-ri-na, con-fes-sa-te! Son di-spo-sto a per-do-

nar. Non par-la-te? vi o-sti-na-te? non par-la-te? vi o-sti

na-te? Sò ben io quel che ho da far, sò ben io quel che ho da far.

rious textual nature. Brimming with traditional stage gimmicks, buffo roles parody the characters they represent, but they are not simple vocal parodies. High-level vocalism is still required.

From Verdi's opera seria *Ernani,* I have selected a classic sustained segment from the aria "Infelice! e tu credevi," beginning at "Ah, perchè, perchè," and continuing to the conclusion of the voice line. The bass role of Don Ruy Gómez de Silva employs a chromatic andante to express his sorrow at the turn of events. With *Ernani,* his fifth opera, Verdi shows the increasing demands he will make on singers. "Infelice! e tu credevi" has cumulative phrases of long duration, which pass in and out of the zona di passaggio region by means of a syllabified text wedded to melismatic fragments. Vowels

change quickly from front-to-back to back-to-front series, on short melismatic duple figures. The performer should carefully observe the semistaccato and accented markings, contrasting them with the flowing fundamental legato. Rests between phrases are part and parcel of the total expressiveness of this aria, and may not be slighted. Each phrase should be sung fully to its conclusion, to be terminated by a clean release. The silence between phrase segments is as expressive as are sung phrases. The rests never negate the remarkable way Verdi creates the impression of one grand phrase that extends from "Ah, perchè, perchè" to terminate with "ancora il cor!"

There also abound other well-structured velocity vocalises from arias and songs by Purcell, Bach, and Handel that are indispensable to the vocal art. The enterprising instructor and the aspiring artist will consider many of them.

Chapter 8

FURTHER CONSIDERATION OF "RESONANCE" IN BARITONE, BASS-BARITONE, AND BASS VOICES

What actually is meant when a low-voiced male is said to have a "resonant voice"? The term denotes a trained voice that carries easily over an orchestra and reveals chiaroscuro balance ("ring" and "richness"). Every professionally motivated singer hopes to achieve it. How is it accomplished?

Unless the singer understands what forms the chiaroscuro tone, and until he possesses the physiologically and acoustically initiated responses to arrive at it, he will be mostly at sea, constantly in search of an idiosyncratic compass. He (possibly his teacher) will try to invent functions unknown to the rest of mankind. Information regarding the physiologic and acoustic components of the resonant sound should not be regarded as mere extraneous data. It provides an essential factual foundation. Building on that knowledge, the low-voiced male is able to establish kinesthetic responses that are as secure as the tasks he undertakes in everyday living (see chapter 4).

I have learned through experience that singers who have an understanding as to why they aim at certain goals move more quickly and permanently in establishing constancy of resonance than do those who try to decode mysterious, even mystical, language. It is valueless to envisage resonance chambers that do not exist, or to try to direct tone to sounding boards that are not present in the chest or the head. The singer's diaphragm is not lodged in locations unknown to nonsingers. Nor does the diaphragm engage in the activities that many singers try to make it perform (see chapter 3).

Solid techniques are not built on acoustic and physiologic fables. Any distraction may have some short-lived benefit. Mentally directing tone to the big toe may sufficiently divert the singer transitorily so that he will let go of some inefficient control, but its value will be fleeting because it establishes no enduring order. By contrast, factual information is precise and is far less complex and more easily assimilated than are the puzzling, arcane conceptions that deal in unfathomable language. A cardinal premise should be kept in mind: "The voice is a physical instrument and obeys the laws of physiology, and the voice is an acoustic instrument and obeys the laws of acoustics." The vital role of imagery should be reserved for the interpretive imagination (see chapters 12 and 17).

From what does resonance balancing really grow? The singer's resonator tube extends from the internal ligaments of the vocal folds to the edge of the external lips. Depending on body structure, this resonator can be of a relatively long or of a compact nature. The larynx generates all voiced human sound, and the vocal tract serves as its filter. Laryngeally engendered sound has no articulatory value of its own. Without the influence of the resonator system that lies above the larynx, all voiced signals would remain a weak, indiscriminate neutral din. Only as the acoustic chamber (the vocal tract) filters laryngeal reverberations into phonetic sound can communicative speaking and singing result. The buccopharyngeal resonator, from larynx to lips, produces discernible phonetic units.

Unlike the tuning fork, the singing voice is made up of frequency components based on a complex overtone series. The listening ear perceives the lowest frequency as the fundamental pitch. From the fundamental are generated a series of harmonic partials (overtones), some of which exhibit greater acoustic intensity than do others. In the speaking voice, the changing shapes of the resonator tract determine the relationships of harmonic partials and formants (see chapter 4). For that reason, throughout this book, we deal in considerable detail with effects of the lips, the mouth, the jaw, and the tongue, facial expression, positioning of velum and larynx, as they bring into being the recognizable resonator-tube shapes by which vowels, consonants, and voice quality are fashioned. When all of these factors are in synchronization, "resonance" results.

It is possible, from time to time, to experience proprioceptive sympathetic-vibration responses by subjective trial-and-error stimuli, but attempting to induce acoustic phenomena solely through the language of imagined function is hazardous at best. It produces a hit-and-miss success rate. Understanding what produces the singer's formant, and how the complete harmonic balance (voce completa) is accomplished, assures the singer of technical dependability and stability. Much of what follows is intended to help increase the performer's awareness of how resonant voice is achieved.

Chapter 9

MORE ON POSITIONING
OF THE LARYNX

During speech, the laryngeal position tends to fluctuate slightly, because the tongue, the hyoid bone, and the larynx function as an anatomical unit. At passaggi pivotal points, the larynx ought to stay in a relatively stable position, without conscious manipulation. It has been previously pointed out that inexperienced male singers tend to elevate the head and chin (hence the larynx) for pitches that lie beyond speech range. In so doing, they inhibit the internal adjustment of the vocal ligaments and the vocalis muscle that should occur in ascending pitch. Timbre then remains "chest" dominant, and the production sounds "pushed," as in calling or shouting, at which time the head is elevated (see chapter 1).

An equally pejorative but contrasting consequence of an elevated larynx is apparent in the emasculated, microphone voice so characteristic of some current male commercial entertainment styles. In the latter cases, the connection between the larynx and the breath-control system is purposely disjointed so that the influence of the fundamental and the first formant are greatly reduced. Only a surface sound remains. An alternate show style consists of driving the sound with excessive airflow and nasality, again accompanied by laryngeal elevation. I have friends in the pedagogic community who assure me that these sounds can be made within the confines of healthy vocalism. Because I do not deal with those sounds, and have not studied them in detail, I withhold further comment.

Once again, two opposing viewpoints regarding laryngeal positioning in the training of classical singers must be mentioned, and discarded, because neither is in accordance with physiological freedom. The first asserts that in order to "free" the larynx, the chin and the head—and therefore the larynx—must be lifted upward. It is claimed that the "sword-swallowing position" (elevated chin and head) is ideal for upper-range pitches. But one cannot phonate and swallow at the same time. During swallowing, the larynx ascends and the epiglottis lowers so that food will be deflected to the esophagus. Swords should be kept in scabbards and out of voice studios.

An opposing and equally injurious suggestion is that the larynx must be drastically lowered for each pitch that lies above the speech-inflection range. In actuality, the larynx belongs in a relatively stable position *throughout* the scale, *not* suddenly depressed at register pivotal points. As opposed to shallow breathing, one inhales deeply for classical singing and there is a slight descent of the larynx. This stabilized laryngeal position is crucial to the freely produced resonant sound of the professional baritone, bass-baritone, or bass voice. The singer has to assure a relatively low-positioned larynx if he is to solidify the chiaroscuro phenomenon—a timbre characteristic of the proficient elite singing voice. Research that reports laryngeal elevation for male high-range classical singing is not based on premier-singer subjects.

How can the ideal laryngeal position for singing be determined by an advanced singer working on his own, and how can a moderately low position become habitual? Take the mirror in hand and sing several relatively simple onset exercises, silently renewing the breath between each "attack." The singer has the impression that he only replenishes the small amount of breath used for an onset. One renews breath almost imperceptively.

Check carefully to be certain that the larynx does not rise at the release of each onset and that it does not alter its position as the breath is silently renewed. Breath renewal is taken not from necessity but because one has the freedom to do so. With each clean release, the vocal folds part fully, and energy is renewed. So slight is replenishment that one is hardly aware of having breathed at all. The *position of inhalation* is maintained throughout the series of onsets. Note an indispensable rubric: "The release *is* the new breath." In summary, the larynx remains in a steady position at initial inhalation, at phrase release, and during the renewal of breath energy.

In most male heavy-duty physical activity unrelated to the singing voice, as energy is increased, the larynx assumes a slightly lower posture. Although this is partly the case for energetic singing as well, it is unnecessary to force the larynx downward, as in the yawn, in order to "cover" the tone. With proper breath preparation the larynx finds a natural stabilized lower position. The pharynx also undergoes some additional expansion without conscious attempts to rearrange it. There is no need for further attempts to "open the throat" or to "spread the pharyngeal wall." "Space" is already there. Upon inhalation, one senses "openness" without consciously engendering it. Natural spatial adjustment and realignment commensurate with the poised larynx—along with the airflow—create a feeling of openness. At best, localized effort to open the throat, or to increase pharyngeal space, feels like a foreign object has been lodged in the throat.

Securing Laryngeal
External-Frame Support

Traditional international techniques of singing wisely draw attention to the maintenance of the axial position and to the necessity for alignment of head, neck, and shoulders (see chapter 16). In so doing, they deal indirectly with the external musculature of the larynx, best known as the laryngeal external-frame function, at which we now look in greater detail.

Major external-frame muscles of laryngeal support include the sternocleidomastoid, the splenius capitis, the semispinalis capitis, the scaleni, and the trapezius muscles. Recent research examines the activity patterns of neck muscles during classical singing (Petterson, 2005). Conclusions are in line with historic pedagogical external-frame support axioms:

> We conclude that STM [sternocleidomastoideus] and SC [scalenus] showed correlated activity patterns during inhalation and phonation by classical singers. Second, substantial muscle activity was observed in PN [posterior neck region] during inhalation and phonation. . . . The activity of all neck muscles was markedly elevated when singing in the highest pitch.

The sternocleidomastoids can elevate the sternum, which action at inhalation increases the anterior-posterior diameter of the thorax. Retention of the inspiratory position during long phrases offers regional support to the larynx. Through the agency of appoggio breath-management, the sternum and the thorax are able to preserve a large percentage of their inhalatory postures.

When performing operatic literature, especially in lengthy and powerful phrases, singers use as much as 100 percent of available vital capacity. This clearly means that greater expansion of the ribcage takes place among professional singers than is common for other phonatory activities such as speaking.

A word of caution is in order. There must be a reasonable balance among the muscles that contribute to the external-frame support of the laryngeal mechanism. Excessive tension—hyperfunction—in one muscle group can cause slackness—hypofunction—in others, leading to vocal fatiguing. Such imbalance manifests itself particularly in the sternocleidomastoids, which must never be allowed to act independently of their neighbors. The posterior neck muscles need to counteract the essential action of the sternocleidomastoids (see chapter 17).

Petterson and Westgaard (p. 240) offer further comment on the location and the activity of the posterior cervical (back of the neck) muscles:

> The posterior cervical muscles consist of four layers. The first layer is formed by the trapezius muscle, the second and third layers are mainly

formed by the splenius capitis and semispinalis capitis muscles, respectively, and the fourth layer is formed by small muscles located between the occipital bone and the first two cervical vertebrae. . . . Pilot studies had shown that muscle activity varied with loudness when performing.

The larynx lodges between the large and usually well-defined paired sternocleidomastoid muscles that serve as external pillars of the neck, and that in most physiques are readily visible when the head is turned to the side while at the same time the sternum remains poised in a straightforward position. Consciousness of firm muscular anchorage of the larynx during singing led to an expression of the Italian school: *appoggio della nuca* (support of the nape of the neck).

Nuchal muscles are located at the base of the skull and tend to be overlooked in modern-day voice pedagogy, yet they contribute to laryngeal stability. They can be fully operative only when the general carriage is poised and the larynx appropriately low. As affirmed by Petterson and Westgaard, the upper trapezius is logically considered among the muscles of the posterior neck region. Posteriorly, the trapezius and the capitis muscles lend assistance in achieving the noble posture that permits the larynx to lie in the position essential to the chiaroscuro timbre of the classical singing voice. It is not possible to maintain a low, supported larynx if the body sags, or if imbalances exist between the head, the neck, and the torso.

Some singers feel that sincerity or intimacy of communication call for a nodding head. They appear compelled to move the head up and down for dramatic emphases. In such cases, the larynx is placed at a functional disadvantage. Noble posture and stance make possible the proper external-frame support of the larynx.

As pointed out earlier, "chest" timbre involves the vocalis muscles. In contrast, elongation of the vocal bands and the diminution of vocalis-muscle activity influence the quality of sound commonly known as "head voice" or "light mechanism." These registration events can be ironed out only if the total instrument—the body—is alert and properly positioned.

Some voice pedagogies deny the existence of registers. Others find as many as seven. As we have seen, historic pedagogy generally speaks of three registers, about which further comment is in order:

Register 1. *voce di petto* (*voix de poitrine, Bruststimme,* chest voice)
Register 2. *voce mista* (*voix mixte, gemischte Stimme, voce media,* mixed voice)
Register 3. *voce di testa* (*voix de tête, Kopfstimme,* head voice)

Register 2 designates the middle of the range of the singing voice, the voce media, the passage zone that lies between so-called chest and head registers (see chapter 1). It results from the graduated processes of vocal-fold stretching, and the appropriate diminishing of vocalis-muscle involvement.

Unlike the singing community, the discipline of voice research identifies only two chief registers: modal and falsetto (a third, vocal fry, plays no role in professional vocalism). In the scientific community, the term "modal" encompasses the speech-inflection range; the term "falsetto" refers to the extended range that lies above most spoken pitch. As noted earlier, when singers use the term falsetto they refer to the imitation of female timbre in the male voice. Standard voice pedagogy designates a recognizable timbre, mixed voice, between what the voice scientist calls modal and falsetto functions.

Only vowel modification and corresponding breath management permit the unified chiaroscuro and avoid the division of the scale into distinctly audible registers. External frame support for the larynx is essential to this procedure.

Stabilizing the Larynx

The larynx is suspended from the hyoid bone, to which the base of the tongue is attached. As the body of the tongue changes position to accommodate the production of front and back vowels, some slight movement of the larynx transpires, but excessive up and down laryngeal motion indicates laryngeal instability. Any movement of the larynx during singing should scarcely be externally visible. There must be equilibrium among the muscle groups—the laryngeal elevators and the laryngeal depressors (which respectively raise and lower the larynx). Although it should never be locally fixated, the larynx must remain stable.

As a check for laryngeal stability, at deep inhalation gently place the index finger and one or more neighboring fingers immediately above the thyroid cartilage of the larynx. Be aware of the slight descent of the larynx at inhalation. The larger the larynx, the greater the visible downward movement at inhalation. Initial inhalatory movement will be more apparent with most bass-baritones and basses than with baritones because the larynges of the lower voices generally occupy more space in the neck structure than do those of baritones. The larynx ought not to rise against the lightly placed fingers. Sing several phrases from the literature while observing in the hand mirror that no laryngeal adjustments happen at onsets, releases, or at the renewal of the breath. Avoiding upward movement of the larynx when breath is replenished is essential to laryngeal stability in singing, particularly for male voices.

It was earlier suggested that the excerpting of demanding passages from the repertoire should be part of the daily practice routine. They are useful only if practiced correctly.

Chapter 10

PEDAGOGIC USES OF FALSETTO FOR BARITONE, BASS-BARITONE, AND BASS VOICES

In public performance, no male singer resorts to falsetto timbre unless ill or for a humorous effect. Falsetto can occasionally be useful in marking (see chapter 17). It should be reiterated that attempting to substitute imitative female sound (falsetto) for legitimate male quality is not a main route of elite vocalism. However, pedagogic uses of falsetto can be productive.

Unless he suffers from an unhealthy condition, the male who lacks a falsetto simply has not yet learned to use it. No matter how faint it may sound initially, with repetition falsetto timbre will stabilize itself. In falsetto production, the elongation of the vocal folds is identical to that assumed by the folds in legitimate male voice (voce piena) but the closure mechanism is not yet fully operative. Nonreinforced falsetto is fashioned by somewhat slacker vocal-fold closure than what happens in vital, resonant sound. For that reason, in the case of the young low-voiced male who tends to press the vocal folds when onsetting in the passage zone, patterns that go from falsetto to voce piena (the natural full male sound) can be of assistance in freeing the voice.

EXERCISE 10.1A

In the first half of exercise 10.1a, beginning in full falsetto mode, using any vowel, the baritone sings a descending A_4–G_4–$F\sharp_4$–E_4–D_4 (5–4–3–2–1) sequence. He remains in falsetto timbre throughout, including the fermata on D_4. In the second half of the exercise, he repeats the falsetto pattern; without interruption, he switches from falsetto to voce piena timbre after arriving at the fermata.

There are two approaches to transitioning from falsetto to full voice: (1) allow the register change to be suddenly apparent, at which moment the closure mechanism is instantly brought into play; and (2) bridge the transition so as to minimize any sudden awareness of a switch in quality. For some persons, one way may be easier, but both methods should be practiced until achievable over time. In the process, subtle laryngeal flexibility is established.

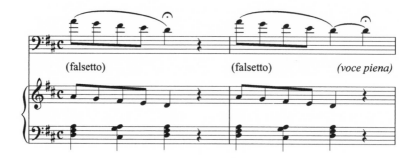

Exercise 10.1a

EXERCISE 10.1B

Moving to the tonality of D♭, the same procedure described earlier is followed.

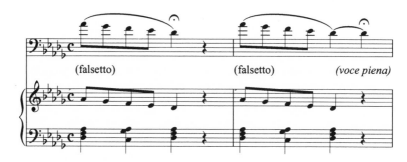

Exercise 10.1b

EXERCISE 10.1C

The transition note is now moved lower. Sensation may differ as the tonality is altered, but the procedure remains. Neighboring keys are critical to the transition from falsetto to voce piena timbres for the low-voiced male. Near tonalities should become equally comfortable with time and practice.

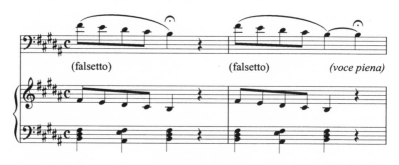

Exercise 10.1c

The exercise can be shortened through a descending pattern accomplished in several neighboring keys.

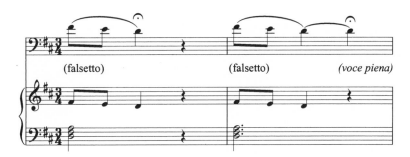

Exercise 10.2a

Exercise 10.2b

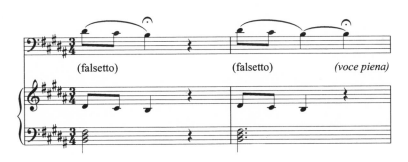

Exercise 10.2c

EXERCISE 10.3A

Exercise 10.3a begins with a 5–4–3–2–1 descending pattern in the tonality of D. At the fermata attach a downward arpeggio to serve as a coda for transitioning from falsetto to voce piena timbre. It ought to be accomplished in a single breath. After a breath renewal, reonset on

F♯₄, remaining in falsetto through pitches 3–2–1. Make the transition from falsetto to voce piena on the fermata note D₄. Without breath interruption, finish the descending arpeggio in full voice.

Exercise 10.3a

EXERCISE 10.3B

The same exercise is moved to the tonality of D♭. These half-note alterations, in changing from falsetto to full, are useful in ironing out falsetto-to-full transitions. They also develop skill in onsetting without tension, and they induce freedom in the closure and open phases of the glottis. Like the passaggio exercises, they are precision drills in registration and liberty of production.

Exercise 10.3b

It is essential to be able to make the falsetto-to-full transitions at various locations in the passage zone. For some singers, conversion is easiest at somewhat higher pitches, for others, at somewhat lower locations. For most low male voices, the key of B is a useful step in this process. All tonalities in the region of the zona di passaggio should be touched (exercise 10.3c).

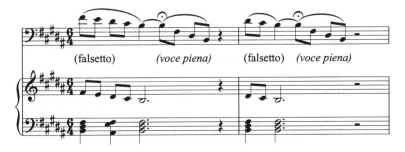

Exercise 10.3c

EXERCISE 10.4A

The first half of exercise 10.4a follows the previous falsetto/voce piena pattern. In the second half of the exercise, after breath renewal, the baritone reonsets at full voice on D_4, with the same ease that he experienced in the transition note from falsetto to full. He sings the entire arpeggio in voce piena.

Exercise 10.4a

EXERCISES 10.4B−C

The same pattern is repeated in lower keys, as in exercise 10.4b and exercise 10.4c.

Exercise 10.4b

Exercise 10.4c

EXERCISE 10.5A

In exercise 10.5a, the baritone returns to the pitch of D_4, which he on-sets in falsetto timbre. Without interruption, he sings a falsetto/voce piena/falsetto sequence.

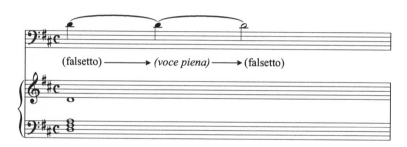

Exercise 10.5a

EXERCISE 10.5B

The same pattern is sung at $D\flat_4$. Practice uninterrupted falsetto-to-voce piena/voce piena to falsetto timbres.

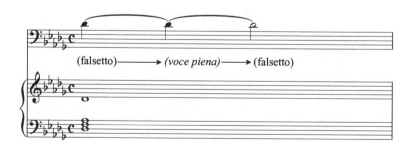

Exercise 10.5b

EXERCISE 10.5C

In exercise 10.5c, the tonality of B becomes the transition point for the falsetto/voce piena/falsetto maneuver.

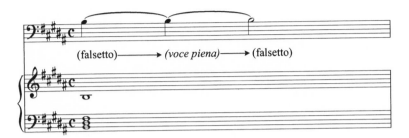

Exercise 10.5c

It is equally rewarding to practice the transition exercises by reversing the order to voce piena/falsetto/voce piena timbre changes.

The bass-baritone may begin the above series in the key of D♭ or in C. The bass may begin the exercises in the key of B. Baritones, bass-baritones, and basses should add neighboring tonalities as skill grows.

If the male singer already has ease in transitioning from falsetto to full—or full to falsetto—he need spend a minimal amount of time on the exercises. However, for the low-voiced male who finds difficulty in shifting from one timbre to the other, these exercises should be practiced daily. They bring about ease of production.

Chapter 11

THE PHENOMENON OF VIBRATO, AN INHERENT COMPONENT OF ELITE VOICE RESONANCE

Reviewers of the singing voice often resort to subjective terminology in describing voice timbre, with metaphors such as "warm," "rich," "full," "thin," "resonant," "dull," "lifeless," "hollow," "colorless," and so on. In general, these expressions refer to the presence or the lack of vibrancy. There is general confusion as to the exact nature of "vibrato." The term is sometimes used pejoratively to include tremolo and oscillation.

Three parameters determine the phenomenon of vibrato: (1) the extent of pitch fluctuation, (2) the temporal rate of pitch alteration, and (3) the intensity and quality of the resultant timbre. In all male voices, pitch excursion associated with vibrato should be approximately a quarter to nearly a half tone. The temporal rate for the baritone vibrato ought to be around 5.5 cycles per second. The bass-baritone and the bass may exhibit slightly slower vibrato rates. In many cases, the bass-baritone and the bass indicate rates similar to those of the baritone. When the pitch excursion is too wide and the temporal rate too slow (falling below five cycles per second), pitch oscillation is extensive. Such timbre is negatively known as a "wobble."

A wobble is the direct result of distortions within the vocal tract. If the jaw is drastically dropped, the pharynx consciously spread, the larynx unduly lowered, and the abdominal wall forced downward and outward, the vibrato rate will be adversely affected. When male low voices have an excessively slow vibrato rate, it easily passes over into held, straight tone.

Conversely, the tremolo (too rapid and too narrow a vibrato excursion) can result from a high laryngeal position together with narrow mouth postures, accompanied by excessive air pressure against the larynx, a result of inward abdominal thrusting. Tremolo long plagued many French baritones. Contrastingly, a number of German low-voiced singers formerly tended to have wider and slower vibrato rates than other international artists.

Straight toning, taken over from the Anglican Cathedral Tone, still remains a problem for certain British singers of both genders. (See R. Miller, *National Schools of Singing*.) Current established singers who pursue successful international careers are, for the most part, not plagued by discernible vibrato aberrations.

Vibrato is a natural component of the elite singing voice. Noted researcher Thomas Shipp (1983, 132) described the vibrato as a "relatively steady impulse that causes the muscles to contract and relax, so that the vocal folds vibrate at frequencies just above or below the target." The nature of a vibrato rate is partly determined by a singer's personal concept of desirable tone.

The teacher who deals with the professionally oriented voice seldom encounters singers who lack vibrancy. However, unlike advanced performers, some youthful singers may lack a vibrato. They must be awakened to its absence and helped to find the freedom that allows vibrato to be present.

In a vibrato-less voice, vibrancy can be induced through the use of short fast agility exercises such as the quickly paced short velocity patterns that grow directly out of the onset (see chapter 7). In most instances, the sustained last note of the 1–2–3 patterns will have at least a touch of vibrancy, pointing the way to vibrato consistency.

Almost without fail, having the beginner imitate animated emotional speech will encourage vibrato. Overcome his inhibitions by playing a foolish children's game: use a melodramatic speech/chant quality, as you would were you to childishly threaten, "I am a ghost, and I'm going to get you!" The student returns the playful threat, imitating teacher's vibratoed speech. This simple, silly game has broken down many a young singer's inhibition about initiating unaccustomed sound and alerts him to the experience of vibrato. Emotional speech, such as that delivered by an overwrought preacher or excited politician in animated exhortation, easily becomes vibratoed speech.

When professional singers fall into nonvibratoed patterns, it is usually because of technical or stylistic error, not from an inability to produce vibrant sound. In some cases, a conscious decision is made to remove the vibrato, a practice which becomes a pitfall for both legato and intonation.

Some singers habitually begin each legato phrase with a straight, vibrato-less onset, reintroducing vibrato as the phrase continues. However, if the initial note is customarily sung straight, the subsequent notes of the phrase are only with difficulty turned into vibrant tone. The singer should be reminded that unless the tone is vibrant, there can be no perception of resonance. Straight-tone onsetting, routine among a few noted lieder singers, rapidly becomes cloying and mannered. There is no stylistic justification for this procedure. It is naïve to sing a lied with a repetitive incursion of straight sound intended as an expressive device, or as vocal coloration. Nor is there supportive evidence that Baroque opera performers made use of straight-tone as their primary vocal quality.

Post–World War II Wagnerian singers often began with vibrato-less onsets, a style that fortunately has lost ground among today's skilled Wagnerian singers. In casting his operas, Wagner employed leading artists of the French, Italian, and Romantic-German opera repertoires, with a few notable exceptions. There is no evidence that they forsook vibrato when turning to the new Wagnerian declamatory style.

Both the advanced preprofessional and the professional baritone must guard against the intrusion of straight tone into sustained phrases and on melismatic passages. A noted coach of international artists of the mid-twentieth century remarked that if, within a ten-second phrase, a single syllable is sung with straight-tone quality—even though all the notes of the phrase are bound together—the perception of legato has been broken. Legato has to do not only with the binding of one note to the next, but with constancy of vibrato—that is, with the "resonance" that links them. "The vibrancy of one note ignites the next" and "It is not difficult to sing from one note to another as long as they are joined by vibrancy" are adages of the Lamperti School. Vibrancy is present in a well-sung pitch, because prephonatory tuning establishes full resonance at the exact moment the phonation commences.

Straight-tone onsetting happens because the singer produces sound either through the false assumption that he is communicating intimacy or because he fails to conceive pitch accuracy before the moment of phonation. Accurate prephonatory tuning, by contrast, involves a split-second mental process. Straight onsets chiefly happen because the singer's ear reacts slowly in conjuring up the targeted pitch. Before the pitch is sung, in a split second the musical ear must conceive of the sound, landing precisely on the desired pitch. This is known as prephonatory tuning. Research based on the phonations of both premier and less-established singers indicates that a competent singer perceives accurate pitch at the exact moment of its production, whereas the less skillful "ear" takes somewhat longer to target the pitch center. Precise onsetting indicates instantaneous coordination among acoustic and breath-management factors. Straight-tone onsets generally begin slightly under the pitch center.

Unintended straight-tone onsetting may occur on a phrase that begins with a vowel. As a corrective practice device, the insertion of a bilabial consonant such as /m/ (also /b/) to serve as pilot to the vowel may solve that problem. The singer is made aware of vibrancy and retains it when he drops the consonant and reonsets with the vowel.

Pitch centering is guaranteed when the level of breath energy is proportionate to the demands of the pitch and the phoneme. Only when the vibrato is present does the tone gain freedom. In a clear-cut onset, airflow and vocal response to the airflow are instantaneously coordinated.

Straight-tone often unintentionally happens on the briefer notes of a phrase, creating a kind of limping legato with a loss of forward direction. This is particularly the case in compound rhythms, such as 6/8, 9/8, and 12/8, with the alternation of eighth and quarter notes: the quarter notes are sung vibrantly, while the connecting shorter eighth notes go straight. Similar error plagues patterns of dotted-quarter/eighth notes, with the long dotted notes vibrant, the brief notes straight.

Vibrato interruption crops up in the juxtaposition of long and short inter-vallic leaps. If a note before an intervallic leap begins straight, the upper note regains vibrancy slowly, if at all. Nonvibrant intervallic jumps are disjunc-tively percussive, and legato is negated.

The insertion of an /h/ in order to articulate the gruppetti of each melisma impairs line and timbre. Nor is it necessary to adjust the vibrato rate to the speed of the melismatic passage being sung (as one influential pedagogy manual advocates), because vibrato is perceived not as a pitch variant of an equal number of fluctuations on each note of the running passage but as timbre that is distributed over an entire phrase. Melismas form the basis of male bravura arias. To sing them with straight tone destroys the intensity they were meant to create.

To provide contrast, straight toning may be introduced as a vocal col-oration, but rarely, and always only intentionally. Straight toning, under the guise of sophisticated phrase sculpting, is mostly disadvantageous.

Vibrato-less singing is not a part of the elite vocalism of the opera, oratorio, and artsong literatures. Undesirable vibrato rates are caused by vocal folds that lose tonicity and fail to offer the essential response to airflow. A vibrato-less tone lacks the presence to maintain itself in a sizeable hall. What worked well in the rehearsal room or the recording studio is not transferable to hall ambience.

One recalls the famous baritone who was well known for his numerous recordings of the standard lied repertoire, all of which demonstrated great sensitivity and finesse. In the recording studio, he often relied on low-dynamic straight-tone production to effect vocal coloration. Yet when the same litera-ture was programmed for recital in a large hall, the same baritone had to forgo most of his straight-tone strategies in order to be audible. Some audi-ence members who knew the famous artist's voice only from his copious recordings were disappointed at the more vital resonant sound he had to use in order to match the acoustics of the large concert hall. "He doesn't sound like his recordings!" He also did not rely on straight tone in his successful opera career.

Straight toning for subtle effects overlooks the fact that messa di voce and dynamic alteration can be achieved while the core of the singing voice is re-tained. Vocal coloration does not require frequent departure from the voce completa (complete voice) timbre. Vibrato is an inherent ingredient of what public and music critic alike term "a resonant voice." Vibrato is an indicator of a healthy production.

Chapter 12

ESTABLISHING TECHNICAL
SECURITY (TRUSTING THE BODY)

Some singers confidently look forward to performance, whereas others experience stress as curtain time draws near. Performance nerves are seldom isolated occurrences. A healthy, technically secure singer, when publicly performing literature appropriate to his voice and to his communicative abilities, experiences excitation but rarely undergoes preperformance anxiety. He has dependable technical and emotional anchors at his disposal (see "Dealing with Performance Anxiety" in chapter 17).

Ill health seriously affects the quality of any singing instrument. When a singer is ill and his body cannot respond to what he has systematically ingrained, he has every reason to feel anxious. One of the most difficult decisions a singer has to make is whether his physical condition will permit him to accomplish what he so well knows how to do. Especially in European theaters, it is customary to meet the commitment if possible, with a notice posted that, despite indisposition, the artist will go ahead. The better-than-expected performance that sometimes takes place when illness is publicly announced is probably because part of normal performance pressure has been reduced. In a similar vein, a recitalist often begins to turn in a stellar performance after the occurrence of his first text flub or rhythmic error. The stress for perfection has been reduced. In any event, most singers tend to rank the audience expectancy level beyond what in reality is the case.

For many singers, auditioning is more nerve-wracking than public performance itself. Limited to presenting only an item or two, the singer must be vocally and artistically convincing. For the secure singer, performance is a joyous occasion. Anticipating a review, some singers are stimulated to new heights at premieres, while others do their best at later performances when premiere pressure has been reduced. No matter how beautiful the voice, the professional who has never established a firm technical foundation will always remain an insecure performer. Premier singer biographies often detail a history of struggle year after year, during which new solutions were sought. Finally there came the day when the artist learned to cast aside intrusive pedagogic theories and put his trust in his instrument.

Fortunate are singers whose pathways have been devoid of up-and-down hurdles. They were either spared the pedagogic technical lottery or were blessed with a native capacity for keeping in touch with the kinesthetics of the body. Akin to the natural athlete, they enjoy *"Sängerischesgefühl,"* a German opera-theater term that means "a feel for singing." From such artists we learn a major performance rule: "Trust the wisdom of the body."

Two factors must be kept in mind: (1) each individual voice shares a commonality of function with every other voice; (2) there is an individuality of physical structure, and a unique creative psyche that sets each voice apart from all others. A confident singer will learn to combine factually based tonal concepts with his own personal imaging. (That's why pedagogy must not be built on imaginative function, but on what is knowable, and on what can be actually assimilated and communicated [see chapter 16]). We now consider more closely the ways an individual can arrive at knowledge best described as "The Wisdom of the Body."

The Wisdom of the Body

How It Feels *(Sensation)*

Avoiding confusion between the source and the sensation of sound is the key to vocal well-being. A singer knows how it feels when everything is working right. When that happens, the three main generators of the singing voice— breath management, laryngeal freedom, and the resonator tube—are in balance. In a nutshell: *What happens with the breath must match what happens at the larynx and what occurs in the resonator tract.*

If the singer believes that tone is formed somewhere where it is not physically possible, for example in the sinuses, or in an imaginary dome above the soft palate, or "up-and-over" (one cannot help enquiring "up-and-over what?"), or in the forehead, or down the spine, the singer is asking the body to do what cannot be done. Despite bogus attempts at localized control, a talented singer will manage to produce some desirable timbre, but the costs in efficiency and security may take a heavy toll.

It is sad to say that some premier singers sing well, not because of, but in spite of, their training. In the excitement of the performance they put aside the things they have been told to do, and simply let the voice work, trusting to what the body knows. The kinesthetic sense permits most of life's activities and is best described as "natural grace." We do not have to engage the mind or muscle groups to command actions that are second nature—walking, running, sitting, standing, or lying down. We leave that to our kinesthetic sense—to the wisdom of the body. Such wisdom is indispensable to the security of the singer. Recall Giovanni Battista Lamperti's dictum: "Controlled singing feels uncontrolled."

Technique underlies elite singing, but must itself never become a public performer. Technical concentration is brought to consciousness only rarely during the course of a public appearance. It must not serve as a brake on what the body has assimilated. As in any sport or art that calls for highly coordinated physical action, a technical monitor subconsciously operates alongside the kinesthetic sense. Methodology should not get in the way of natural grace. On stage, conscious technique is called on only when specific musical variation or dramatic impact requires. The seasoned singer focuses on sound, word, drama, and communication.

A singer who has breathing skills, who has a good perspective on how his voice responds to airflow, and who understands what actually happens within the resonator system is free to express himself.

How It Sounds (Internal Listening)

A singer relies both on inner and outer hearing. Hungarian researcher Georg von Békésy asserted that we listen approximately 50 percent internally and 50 percent externally. Other researchers believe that most of what we perceive of our own sound comes from internal listening, as the consequence of sympathetic vibration among the cavities of the head. When the *chiaro* portion of the chiaroscuro is in balance with the *oscuro* part, regions of the face register sympathetic vibration (see chapter 4).

The bony structures and cavities of the head, which include the hard palate, the skull, the sinuses, the zygomatic arch, and the forehead, serve as excellent conductors of sympathetic vibration. They may feel like resonators, but they are not so significantly. Their responses differ substantially from singer to singer (see chapter 8).

How It Sounds (External Listening)

There is a school of singing that claims a singer cannot hear himself sing. It is believed that he ought not to listen to his sound as he produces it. Clearly, the singer or speaker does not hear his own voice as do his listeners, but certainly he is able to distinguish among the wide variety of sounds he is capable of producing. In fact, the ability to monitor one's sound, both internally and externally, is essential to a solid technique.

External hearing is dependent on the construction and condition of the complex ear organ and on room acoustics. Matters of health, ambient noise, and acoustic circumstances can affect the sensations of both internal and external hearing.

Ear cupping is a false friend. By enhancing awareness of upper harmonic partials, it misleadingly augments the perception of higher formants and makes the sound appear brighter than it actually is. It produces the same effect as singing into the corners of a room, or as vocalizing in a shower enclosure.

In a stage setting, one hears not only one's own voice but also the high decibel levels of singers around one. A trained singer learns to listen both internally and externally, never allowing his own voice to be altered by the surrounding voices.

The seasoned opera singer manages to finesse stage directions so that his voice is almost never directed away from the audience. Professional artists are masterful at not deploying sound to the wings, regardless of the staging directions. No matter how small the hall, contact with the house and the conductor needs to be maintained. Proper stage-deportment techniques allow full rapport with fellow singers on stage while assuring audience connection.

If there is a temporary hearing impairment, as with a head cold, the singer needs to adjust his external listening. He should also, if at all possible, avoid air travel when suffering from closed ears, or from a heavy upper respiratory infection.

What It Looks *Like (Visual Aspects of the Vocal Instrument)*

Most musical instruments can be held or manipulated. Because the singing voice cannot, it is often described as "the hidden instrument." Although it is true that the complete buccal-pharyngeal resonation system is not outwardly detectable, much of it actually *is*. We can see the lips, the mouth, and the apex of the tongue (see chapter 4). Also outwardly observable are the laryngeal location, posture, and stance that produce external-frame support (see chapter 9). The relationship of the larynx to the sternum and to the pectorals can be perceived as well.

The serratus muscles (dorsal muscles that arise from the ribs and vertebrae) are familiarly known as "the boxer's muscles." Although they are not respiratory muscles, they help position the thorax; as does the great latissimus dorsi that covers a large area of the back. Some British twentieth-century manuals on singing claimed the serratus and latissimus dorsi muscles as important to inhalation. Those muscles are central as postural and stance muscles but do not directly participate in inhalation. Latissimus dorsi is chiefly activated in sudden forced exhalation, as in coughing. Actions of the serratus and latissimus dorsi groups can both be viewed surfacely.

The bundle of muscles that surrounds the mouth and the lips is externally visible. Every emotion is associated with some specific facial gesture. A singer should know how each expression appears and how each one feels. He ought to memorize the sensations and be able consciously to duplicate them. In short, a singer should know what his face looks like while he is singing. Some singers are hesitant to watch themselves in a mirror or on videotape. "I don't want to see myself" is a common comment. The singer seems to forget that his audience is aware of what his face expresses or fails to express. Know what your face looks like when you are singing. Everybody else does.

There are not an unlimited number of facial expressions. For much of the time, a pleasant facial expression serves the text and drama. Fundamentally, emotion is an expression of either positive or negative sentiment. Not to differentiate between the two is to belie the text, but it is unnecessary to indulge in the mugging to which various singers fall prey.

Body language has to match the sentiments being expressed (see "The Role of Physical Quietude in Classical Singing" in chapter 16). Nothing is more damaging to communication than a lazy bearing during the performance of vital literature. It is equally disturbing to see a singer who never breaks stance, but who seems cemented to a spot in the curve of the pianoforte. The habit of singing with one hand placed on the piano's lid (or just beneath it, if the lid is raised) binds the singer to a static pose. It is totally illogical for a singer to brace himself with one hand on the piano as he sings an opera audition. There are no pianos on opera stages on which to hang.

How it sounds, how it feels, and what it looks like provide the singer with the feedback he most needs. All are of equal importance.

Chapter 13

DEVELOPING AN INDIVIDUAL
TONAL CONCEPT

The attributes of beautiful singing never happen willy-nilly. They are universally identifiable and they are teachable and learnable. Freedom of the imagination depends on the stability of a singer's tonal concept. It is essential to renew the exploratory, interpretive spirit at each performance. Technical problems should be dealt with long in advance, so that during performance the imagination may be channeled to communication (see chapter 17).

A complete tonal concept remains elusive for some singers, at times even for those who have achieved occasional notable successes. Some performers are inconsistent about retaining a reliable ideal sound. What went well in the coaching lesson and in the practice room remains shrouded in mystery; one performance may be satisfactory, the next less so. By insistence on the well-coordinated sound, am I recommending that there be only a single color for the voice? Of course not! How can the drama be enacted unless one varies the interpretation? However, the wise singer adheres to a principle enunciated by great technician and interpreter Alfredo Kraus: "Never let the text or the drama rob you of the beauty of your voice."

Over the course of a single performance, a baritone may be called on to express love, despair, joy, anger, nostalgia, regret, and triumph. He presents all of these sentiments with a single vocal instrument but with shadings of timbre. He does not do so by altering his technique, but by adapting it to the dramatic situation. Rigoletto does not use one technique for taunting Monterone, another for tenderness with Gilda, and yet another in his dark dealings with Sparafucile. He alters phrasing and dynamics, and he handles each mood differently, but he does not turn his voice into three different instruments or three disparate productions. He adjusts tonal balances to match the emotions of the situation, but he does not abandon his basic tonal concept.

With the recording industry outburst of the mid-twentieth century came stylistic awakening, particularly in the field of the lied. Commendable though this movement was, it dangerously flirted with the "lieder complex," whereby the individual artist exhibited his personal conception of sensitivity to the detriment of the composer. Voice distortion is not vocal coloration. The call for "ugly sound" in any role or lied is extremely limited (see chapter 11).

A performer who feels compelled to express his feelings by stringing together unrelated vocal sounds runs the peril of losing the core of his voice. He should keep in mind that expressive singing is not accomplished by parodistic means. There are times when a momentary departure from the nucleus of his sound may be desirable, but he should seldom go far from his native timbre. The buffo bass will bluster, and the romantic baritone will woo, but each does so with his own true voice. This is not a granting of license for inexpressive singing, but a reminder that great artists use the beauty of their voices to capture a wide range of emotions.

How is a tonal ideal established? The singer must hear fine singing in order to establish a tonal concept of his own. This does not mean that he imitates the great voices to which he listens. But a young baritone who has only a vague idea as to the quality of sounds produced by noted baritones of the past and present is working in a vacuum. Most singers have well-developed imitative powers, yet the young male singer must never mimic a sound that is inappropriate to his youthful voice. On any given pitch, a trained singer can make three or four distinct timbres, none of which is patently ugly. But one of those sounds will be more in accordance with the singer's instrument than are the others. That quality must be identified and stabilized.

For half a century it has been my privilege to be associated with a number of emerging young artists, with well-established professionals who perform in major venues, and with promising voice performance majors at premier schools of music. I have asked each singer who began working with me, "Who are your favorite singers?" Inevitably, the most promising of them were familiar with past and present premier voices, based on both live and recorded performances. There can be no doubt that potential professional singers need to be aware of elite vocalism. (For some models, see appendix 1.)

One corrective pedagogic approach requests that the singer, in order to distinguish good versus bad vocalism, first produce tension-generated sounds, then attempt to eliminate them. However, one must be able to recognize and experience how to produce free sound before it can be compared with stressful sound. Student and teacher should consistently strive for the most complete model, not for less-than-ideal sound.

A student ought to be able to rely on his teacher's ability to diagnose and prescribe. The best means available is the teacher's own ability to produce a well-balanced sound. If the teacher is female, for her male students she can show a well-produced sound with her own instrument. She should rarely, if ever, use her female chest voice to demonstrate male-voiced singing, particularly if she is still an active performer. A tenor teacher uses his own complete timbre with his low-voice students. An aging teacher may be restricted to demonstrating in a more limited range. There is little danger that a singer will imitate the teacher's sound, be that teacher male or female. The student singer will recognize the principles of freely produced vocalism. Caution is in order. If the modeling is bad, so will be the results. If the teacher is a non-singer, modeling is not an option, of course. Historically, some noted voice teachers were themselves not singers. Yet, a teacher who himself or herself is performance experienced has a distinct advantage.

An instructor must be able to point out which sounds come from unhampered vocal-fold action and which are manufactured or incomplete. Old muscular responses must be rebuilt to comply. To accomplish that end, the teacher needs to diagnose faults and prescribe solutions through the specificity of language (see appendix 2). Establishing a tonal ideal is a gradual process. Teacher and student should not be surprised that it requires time and patience.

Chapter 14

DYNAMIC CONTROL, *MEZZA VOCE,* AND THE *MESSA DI VOCE*

With most young male singers, it is difficult to adhere immediately to every subtle dynamic indicated in the song and opera literatures, particularly in and above the zona di passaggio region. Mezza voce (literally, half voice) is a sophisticated skill. As Giovanni Battista Lamperti maintained, mezza voce tone should in all respects be the same as forte, except be softer. Legitimate mezza voce requires an increase—not a decrease—in the appoggio activity. A well-known pedagogic rubric: "Sing piano, support forte."

The messa di voce is markedly different from mezza voce. With the messa di voce, the phrase begins at *p* or *pp* dynamic level, gradually advances to *f* or *ff*, and then returns to *p* or *pp* intensity. The messa di voce has long been considered a test as to how well breath emission and vocal-fold approximation are coordinated. In a 1782 treatise titled "Mr. Tenducci to His Scholars," Giusto Ferdinando Tenducci succinctly states: "To sing messa di voce—swelling of the tone—begin pianissimo and gradually increase to forte in the first part of the tone; then gradually diminish to the conclusion of each note."

Noted twentieth-century Italian opera coach Luigi Ricci, who worked with many premier singers of that recent golden age, considered the messa di voce a necessity for the development of dynamic control throughout the singer's range. (His advice is not intended for the beginning student.) Ricci suggested starting with the messa di voce just below the passage zone, gradually raising the pitch over the weeks and months. It was his viewpoint that if, over a period of years, a singer could accomplish the messa di voce maneuver on all lateral and rounded vowels, on every note of his performable scale, he would have passed the final test in technical proficiency.

I think it is wisest to begin with an interrupted messa di voce, in which the true messa di voce is divided into two sections. The baritone, bass-baritone, or bass is advised to onset the tone at as low a dynamic level as possible and to crescendo to as high a forte as he can comfortably produce. He releases the sound at forte level, renews the breath silently, and reonsets at the same forte level. He then diminishes to the quietest level possible. Immediately thereafter, he turns to the true messa di voce, completing the maneuver in a single breath. The two procedures can be graphed as in exercises 14.1 and 14.2.

EXERCISES 14.1 AND 14.2

Exercise 14.1

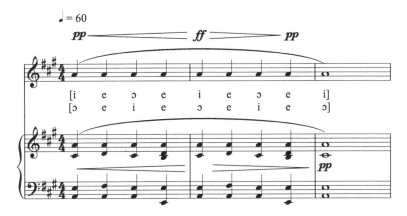

Exercise 14.2

The aim is not to attempt dynamic extremes but to smoothly change from one dynamic to another. Aspirated and light glottal onsets are alternated. To be avoided is any sudden burst of breath energy from piano to forte level. Gradual energization is the goal. It is wrong to assume that a point on the dynamic scale is reached when the singer suddenly "drives in the wedge," as one widely disseminated pedagogic source recommends. Rather, consistency of timbre at all dynamic levels of the exercises is the aim.

There should be an increase in epigastric-umbilical contact during the course of the sustained note, while quality remains constant. The highest level of breath-management activity comes at the concluding pianissimo. Do not use falsetto timbre to practice the messa di voce maneuver. Throughout the exercise, the tone must have voce-completa quality. Mixing breath to reduce volume is to be avoided.

Another pedagogic misconception of the messa di voce is that a singer must begin with piano dynamic in "head voice," shift to "chest voice" for the forte or fortissimo, then return to "head voice" for the diminuendo. On the contrary, any registration shifts must be avoided.

I recommend that male low-voiced singers begin the messa di voce exercises immediately below the first passaggio, gradually raising the pitch (as skill develops) into the passage zone, then ultimately into upper range. Messa di voce is an elite endeavor that takes time to master. An expert singer should eventually be able to accomplish the messa di voce in all registers of the voice. In general, the larger the instrument, the more time required for the messa di voce conquest.

Chapter 15

VOICE VIRUSES (DEALING WITH SOME COMMON PROBLEMS OF MALE LOW VOICES)

Several problems for male low voices that have received passing attention need further elaboration. These "voice viruses" invade chiaroscuro balance, and damage interpretive artistry. A few anti-viral prescriptions may prove useful, particularly in dealing with the young male voice. These descriptive titles are not to be found in historic voice pedagogy!

The Unipeeper (Undersinging)

Forty years ago, it was common for an immature male singer to bring excessive energy and tension to the onset and to the phrase. Today, there is more likely to be a lack of physical involvement. An unformed "peeping sound" pervades many young male voices. This curious change has to do with the musical environment that surrounds today's youthful singer. His listening experiences are chiefly those of popular TV, radio, and rock. (*American Idol* is at the moment the most watched entertainment.) The omnipresence of the microphone in the commercial entertainment world has contributed markedly to undersinging (as well as to yelling). Whatever the appropriateness of most current popular vocalism to the "show" world, it remains disadvantageous to the cultivated singing voice.

Yet another cultural change has its source in the contemporary "Broadway Sound" that has replaced the "musical comedy" singing style of the past, which was not far removed from its classical heritage. Many of today's Broadway producers have little regard for healthy vocalism. Stridency and primitivism replace beauty and ease of production. Producers can always replace worn-out voices with other hopefuls standing in line.

A few simple isometric exercises are helpful in correcting the problem of undersupported singing.

EXERCISE 15.1

Have the student press the palms of the hands firmly together while accomplishing onset exercises. Begin each onset with an increase of hand pressure; silently renew the breath. Repeat a number of times.

EXERCISE 15.2

A related device is also based on the principle of isometric contraction, as in exercise 15.2. Place the elbows outward from the torso, arms akimbo at mid-sternum level, with the fingers of each hand gripped in opposition. While singing onsets, pull outward with the elbows, increasing resistance at the fingers.

The Uniboomer (Oversinging)

Achieving ideal airflow and the proper vocal-fold response to it is a major part of voice training. A common fault, especially for the operatic male singer, is to offer too much vocal-fold resistance to airflow, which causes pressed phonation and a constant bellowing or "booming" quality. What should the optimal balance be? How is tonicity maintained at the same time as freedom?

Phonation is classifiable as (1) breathy, (2) normal, or (3) pressed—states determined by the extent of glottal occlusion. For example, a high degree of breathy phonation pertains in the whisper. Breathiness is also present in hoarseness, because edema (swelling) does not permit firm vocal-fold closure. Extensive gapping between the vocal folds (undersinging) plagues some male singers. When airflow and vocal response to the breath are well coordinated in the healthy voice, breathy quality is eliminated, and the tone is clean and normal.

The opposite error is pressed phonation, in which vocal folds are too tightly occluded. Excessive pressures in the abdominal wall cause most pressed phonation. Questionable maneuvers suggested in some pedagogy sources include the imitation of difficult defecation. (A comparable advice for females is to push downward as in childbirth.) Related recommendations include trying to lift the piano or other heavy objects, or squeezing and tightening the anal sphincter. (I refrain from citing possible unexpected arresting performance consequences.) None of them permit the precise coordination of airflow and vocal-fold approximation required to produce balanced phonation that is neither breathy nor pressed. The clean onset generates such vocal freedom.

Tensions of the thoracic and the abdominal regions induce immediate laryngeal responses. If a singer is customarily relying on the "grunt" (exaggerated vocal-fold closure), introduce the notion of "free-flow phonation." Free-flow phonation is best understood as the reduction of resistance by the vocal folds to the exiting air. Again a caveat is in order. Flow phonation does not mean conscious or audible addition of a breath stream, but easing up on breath pressure and on the weight of the sound. This is essential when entering the zona di passaggio, where mature males often tend to overenergize. Achieving a slenderer timbre while traversing the passage zone frees the singer from building up tension as he enters the upper ranges (see chapter 6). However, he doesn't "relax" everything to achieve it. (See "The Question of Relaxation" in chapter 17.)

The Shatterer (Intermittent Breaking in the Passaggio Region)

Males are faced with a greater need for vowel-modification adjustment and breath management in the passaggio region than are their female colleagues. Cracking—the dreaded "*canard*" or "voice break"—occurs under one of two conditions: (1) the laryngeal support is too slack at pivotal registration points (see "The Unipeeper [Undersinging]"); or (2) pressures are so high that the laryngeal musculature has to shift. The entire mechanism "jumps" to release the accumulating tension (see "The Uniboomer [Oversinging]").

One of the best ways to work on this "fracturing" problem is to start a short exercise pattern such as 5–8–7–6–5 just below the first passaggio point and move it into the passage zone. Lateral and rounded vowels should be alternated. See also exercise 4.8 on page 48.

EXERCISE 15.3

A baritone begins on A$_3$ in the key of D, the bass-baritone at A♭$_3$ in the tonality of D♭, the bass at G$_3$ in C. Proceed upward by semitones through several neighboring keys, increasing the breath support as the transition pivotal points are encountered.

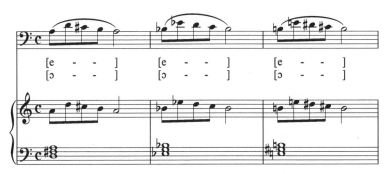

Exercise 15.3

Employing isometric onset exercises in the region of the second pivotal registration point helps alleviate cracking in the passage zone. Dr. Emil Froeschels, known as "The Father of Phoniatrics," devised isometric exercises to bring about better vocal-fold closure without increasing tension. Dr. Friedrich Brodnitz, an eloquent follower of Froeschels, used exercises based on the research of Froeschels. Examples are included in his *Vocal Rehabilitation: A Manual Prepared for the Use of Graduates in Medicine, American Academy of Ophthalmology and Otolaryngology.* There is a primary two-part message in the Froeschels/Brodnitz exercises: (1) chewing and speaking make use of related laryngeal functions; and (2) whenever the arms and the torso are involved in heavy work, the glottis closes more firmly. The following exercises are based on these assumptions. In all of the following exercises there must be no grunting or pressing at the level of the larynx during any portion of their execution.

EXERCISE 15.4. DOWNWARD THRUSTING, AND SPOKEN ONSETTING, IN CONJUNCTION WITH PLOSIVE CONSONANTS

Fists are placed at the level of the sternum. Downward thrusting of the fists is synchronized with spoken phonations. The plosive consonants /p–b–t–d–k–g/ are individually joined to vowels from the /ɑ–e–i–o–u/ series. Downward thrusting and the spoken onset do not alter the axial stance.

EXERCISE 15.5. SUNG ONSETS IN THE PASSAGE ZONE COUPLED WITH VIGOROUS DOWNWARD THRUSTING

Place fists at the sternum, shoulders positioned firmly back. Individual syllables are sung on single pitches in the passage zone, coordinated with downward vigorous thrusts. For example at D_4, the syllable "be" or "pe"; "te" or "de"; "ke" or "ge" is sung as the fists are thrust downward.

EXERCISE 15.6. SINGING PROBLEMATIC PHRASES WHILE EXPERIENCING EXTERNAL RESISTANCE

The singer should stand erect with the shoulders well back and the pectorals positioned well forward. He must be aware of an increase of activity among the head, neck, and torso muscle groups ("The back of the neck feels long, the front of the neck feels short"). Retain the same energized connection between head, neck, and shoulders, arms loosely hanging downward, while singing a difficult passage in the passaggio region where "cracking" occurs. The instructor pulls down evenly and steadily on the singer's forearms during the phrase. The singer resists from a secure axial position. The passage is repeated without the physical action from the instructor.

EXERCISE 15.7. "TUG-OF-WAR"

Exercise 15.7 is a tug-of-war game between the singer and an antagonist (his instructor). Each plants one foot forward beside the corresponding foot of his opponent, with the body weight on his own opposite leg. The fingers of both hands are interlocked with those of his combatant partner. Retaining the axis of head, neck, and shoulders, each tries to pull the other over, while resisting his opponent.

Competitive resistance is exerted, and the mood must be one of enjoyable antagonism. If the instructor is an accomplished singer, he joins in singing the passage while playing the game. The student sings the passage by himself, retaining the same energization, but no longer participating in the game.

EXERCISE 15.8. "CARGO"

The singer places his elbows inward against the sides of the upper torso; arms extended forward, palms up. His outstretched hands and forearms are gradually weighted with books, music scores, or other objects that must be held only through an axial posture of the thorax, the spine, and the torso. The singer retains a noble stance as his arms offer resistance to the gravitational downward pull. The passage is sung with loaded arms; then, without the "cargo."

It is clear that isometric exercises induce firm glottal closure. Notice that one can speak and sing with freedom at the level of the larynx during the application of high-level energization. These exercises make the singer aware of the necessity for contact among the musculatures of the head, neck, and torso.

However, a word of serious caution is very much in order. Isometric exercises are to be reserved for extreme cases, in which normal techniques for securing sustained passages above the zona di passaggio have not proved successful. One or more of these exercises may be effective in eliminating the problem of cracking. They are not a part of regular studio practice but are to be strictly reserved for the relatively advanced singer who has a "shattering" problem in the upper range. I have personally used these exercises rarely, and

I have never used all of them with any single individual. I offer them here in the hope that they will be judiciously applied in extreme cases only.

The Wanderer (Flatting and Sharping)

Pitch vagaries—intonation sometimes above the targeted pitch, sometimes below it—are seldom simply a matter of ear accuracy. They involve technical faults, including straight-toning and fluctuating breath management.

Singing sharp can be caused by too high an airflow as well as by excessive resistance of the vocal folds to the exiting breath. Sharping may be caused by inward tensing of the abdominal wall under the assumption that breath is supported by such action. The closing process of the vocal folds is then too intense and the pitch rises. Sharp singing is inclined to be tremulous; it is exacerbated by high laryngeal positioning.

Flatting may be the outcome of breath slackness, the consequence of insufficiently occluded vocal folds. If a singer is always slightly under pitch, the entire resonance balance is lacking in upper partials. Sometimes a singer will depend so heavily on internal versus external listening that he is unaware of his propensity for nomadic pitch (see chapter 13). He must learn to *listen* to his voice, as well as to produce it. One of the best solutions to the pitch wanderer's problem is to record an aria or song, then to check it back note by note against pianoforte pitches. This heightens awareness of pitch centering and of the need to listen externally as well as internally.

Techniques that emphasize migration of all vowels toward the back-vowel series reduce the chiaro (bright) feature of the voice in favor of the oscuro (dark) aspect. A production that is heavy on first formant resonance has a propensity to lower the pitch, because the upper partials are not sufficiently strong. Even if the fundamental has the correct number of cycles per second, when upper partials are lacking, the perception on the part of the listener is that the pitch has fallen.

As with most vocal faults, there may be a number of contributing factors to uncertain pitch targeting, and the singer who suffers from intonation vagaries should carefully reassess each aspect of his technique.

The Sausage Maker (Nonlegato Singing)

A major emphasis of this book has concerned the ability to sustain a flowing vocal line. "Legare" means to bind together. Legato is an inherent ingredient of sostenuto and of bel canto phrase shaping. The deleterious effect of straight toning on legato has been pointed out (see chapter 13). The intrusion of nonvibrant syllables interrupts the linear flow.

Another detrimental practice is to allow most syllables to fall to a lower dynamic level after their initial onset. The second half of the note ebbs away, dropping off to a lower dynamic level. Such "link sausaging," with sound coming and going, can be graphed thus: <> <> <> <> <>. My wife describes this style of singing as "touch and retreat." At times I have termed it "the revolving door" or the "concertina" school of singing. In the hope of being musical, the singer actually becomes unmusical—precious and pseudo-artistic. The most expressive vocal and musical device in the singer's arsenal is the ability to weave a legato line.

The Univoweler
(Diction Distortion)

Vowel definition is an innate component of the chiaroscuro tone (see chapter 4). Consideration has been directed to using vowels and consonants to achieve resonance balance. Attention is now turned to the singer who relies on "the universal vowel."

A damaging concept holds that in order for the tonal quality to remain consistent, all vowels are to be sung though a basic mouth shape. It was once my experience to replace a teacher whose students, male and female, had been taught to form all vowels through the shape of the phoneme /œ/. They were told (with some basis in acoustic fact) that /œ/ includes acoustic elements of both the front and back vowel series, thus producing a more complete harmonic balance among all vowels. Diction perception was, of course, greatly reduced, and they looked as though they had been nibbling persimmons, or were imitating guppies.

Other pedagogies have promoted yet some other single mouth posture through which all vowels are to be filtered. Enunciation is cast aside in favor of a universal vowel posture. Such admonitions are in conflict with the historic "si canta come si parla" maxim. Diction is then a lost cause.

Diction is not something that is put on after basic sound has been established in the singing voice. One teacher of considerable repute complained that contest judges unkindly mentioned that her singers were basically unintelligible. Her justification was that she had spent so much time on technique that there was never sufficient time to get around to diction! Diction, on the contrary, is the generator of well-balanced timbre and the initiator of the acoustical aspects of voice technique. Vocalization is fundamentally vowelization. An Italian adage expresses it well: "Chi pronuncia bene, canta bene" (who enunciates well, sings well).

The Sluggard (Sighing and Yawning)

One widely dispersed precept (the yawn/sigh technique) aims to reduce vocal-fold tension by coupling yawning with sighing. Neither is appropriate to the vitality of the opera stage or the recital hall. Both lessen muscle tonicity essential to the athletic singing of classical voice literature. Sighing causes high airflow rates, and sustained yawning produces ingolata timbre. Sometimes it is suggested that a singer who "oversupports" should consciously introduce sighing, thereby adding a mixture of breath to the tone. Although the suggestion may bring some immediate relief, there is danger that excessive airflow will become habitual.

The Uniregistrant (The No-Register Singer)

There are those who claim that registers are the invention of voice teachers. Perhaps they mean that a unified scale has no discernible registration breaks. Unfortunately, ignoring the events of registration inevitably leads to "open" singing (see chapter 16). A baritone, bass-baritone, or bass singer unaware of registration events cannot produce refined vocalism. Much of technical work lies in learning to negotiate registers (see chapter 5). Ignoring registration of the voice is especially detrimental in the low male voice. Unless the modified scale is achieved, the classical literature of the singing voice remains unrealizable.

I have termed these frequently encountered errors "viruses" because they often are transmitted by well-meaning pedagogues. They disrupt the principles of healthy, free vocalization. Suggested cures for these viruses are imbedded in the technical exercises outlined in this book.

Chapter 16

CONTRIBUTING TO PERFORMANCE
EFFECTIVENESS

Obtaining the Axial Position

I have maintained that posture and stance are crucial to fine singing. But in attempting to maintain an axial position, a singer may become rigidly fixated so that involuntary tensions are introduced. Several long-accepted practices to reduce tension are variations of the earlier encountered silent Farinelli maneuver, which is now joined to singing (see chapter 3).

EXERCISE 16.1. APPLYING THE
FARINELLI EXERCISE IN SINGING,
WHILE LYING DOWN

The singer lies on his back, as in the Farinelli maneuver. It is best that a pillow or two be positioned under the head to ensure that the larynx is not elevated. Breathe normally, feeling as relaxed as possible. Place one hand on the front of the abdominal wall, the other at the side of the lower ribs. Notice the expansion that occurs at inhalation. Next, lengthen this inhalatory gesture, retaining it for as long as is comfortable.

There is no sensation of "holding the breath"; one simply suspends the respiratory process. Breathing should be quiet and regular. Lips ought to be parted so that there is no holding back of the breath by the lips during the process of respiration. Aim for easy suspension of the breath, its measured exhalation, and quiet breath renewal. After a series of silent respiratory cycles, sing a few brief onset exercises, followed by legato phrases of varying lengths, chosen from literature excerpts.

EXERCISE 16.2. APPLYING THE FARINELLI EXERCISE IN SINGING, WHILE SEATED

The singer sits on the floor in native-American fashion, legs akimbo, with hands crossed at the sacroiliac. Repeat the silent breathing exercises; follow them with sustained sung phrases.

EXERCISE 16.3. APPLYING THE FARINELLI EXERCISE IN SINGING, WHILE KNEELING

Keeping the spine in alignment, the singer kneels, and repeats the process, moving from silent breath pacing to phrases from the literature.

EXERCISE 16.4. APPLYING THE FARINELLI EXERCISE IN SINGING, WHILE STANDING

While singing a sustained phrase, the singer rises to a standing position, maintaining the same axial position that was present when lying, sitting, or kneeling.

EXERCISE 16.5. WALKING TO AND FRO WHILE SINGING PHRASES

Walk slowly backward and forward, remaining in axial posture, while practicing exercises and portions of songs or arias. The singing of a complete song or aria in any of the above positions may prove to be a useful device.

Any baritone who has sung Mercutio's "Queen Mab" aria in Gounod's *Roméo et Juliette* knows that the stage director will have him bouncing and jumping about the stage. What then of insistence on stance and posture? The good news is that there is little that a creative stage director can demand that a well-trained singer cannot deliver. A seasoned performer discovers ways to finesse stage action, pacing movement so as to preserve coordination between good breath-management and physical mobility. He manages rapid breath renewal through the disciplined onset. He has acquired the ability to sustain long phrases through sostenuto exercises. His singing will have been schooled during lying down, kneeling, sitting, standing, and walking. Seldom is a knowledgeable stage director so unreasonable as to request physical distortion at moments of dramatic vocal climax.

The Role of Physical Quietude
in Classical Singing

Body and leg motion, gyrating torso, and hand and arm gesticulation are earmarks of the commercial performance style. Both intimate and animated expressions are confided to the ubiquitous microphone so as to simulate deep feeling and elation. By contrast, the artsong, oratorio, and operatic literatures chiefly demand nobility and tranquility. Sentiments conveyed by the singing voice require more time than those ranted or chattered.

The classical singer should learn to remain physically poised, with an air of serenity. Movement can induce freedom, but it also can become enslaving. In practice sessions, sweeping arm and hand movements may be of use but are meaningless on stage. Habitual gesticulation, weaving from the trunk, and backward and forward body shifting reveal instability. The body must not be at odds with itself, with legs and feet on one plane of action and upper torso, neck, and head on another.

Unrest is expressed through constant motion; composure is manifested by flexible stability. (As one philosopher/theologian expressed it: "The damned are in ceaseless motion.") Quietude begins with good stance and an occasional natural shifting of body weight. When speaking while standing, as expression changes, body weight is transferred from one hip and leg to the other hip and leg by a partial step backward or forward. In trying to keep an erect posture, many inexperienced singers cement themselves to the floor.

Learning to limit physical movement is important to "classical quietude." The small emotive movements natural to all communication should be retained, but phrase rhythm is never to be confused with the regulated pulse or beat of the music. The elite vocalist shuns conducting, directing traffic, praying, carrying invisible buckets of water, brandishing a sword, holding back the dog on his leash, or spraying his audience with a garden hose. Conversely, no singer should look like a statue positioned in the curve of the pianoforte, or "park and bark" in opera.

On the opera stage, undirected movement reduces the verisimilitude of the drama. "The technique of weight shifting is an integral part of producing a believable stage persona" (Miller, 2004, p. 37). The artist incorporates the partial step and its accompanying shift of body weight to give the appearance of looking at, and listening to, his stage peers. He manages a frequent two-thirds-open stance, never losing contact with stage events, with the conductor, or with the house itself. There must be no tinge of "*acting* acting." Movement and gesticulation ought to be within the confines of normal human encounter. The opera singer must learn to walk *out* of rhythm. Body language is of as much importance as is singing tone. Constant movement proves distracting for singer and audience.

Distinguishing between
Resonance and Nasality

As has been pointed out, the nasals /m/, /n/, /ɲ/, and /ŋ/ show acoustic energy in the region of the singer's formant (see chapter 4). It is easy to confuse nasality with the singer's formant. Nasality that is present in any phoneme except a nasal continuant represents a distortion of timbre. Except for the French (and Portuguese) nasal vowels, no vowel contains a nasal component. (The traditional check for nasality was described earlier on page 55.)

Colloquial American speech has so profoundly invaded TV and public life that it is now a major problem for singers. Unless the singer is aware of the frequent intrusion of nasality in the speaking voice, it is difficult for him to eliminate nasality from his singing.

A long-established therapeutic device for detecting nasality in speech is the "Rainbow Passage." This famous paragraph was at one time considered an indispensable check for nasality and other language aberrations. I periodically ask singers to read the passage aloud for me. It may be wise (assuming the teacher has eliminated nasality from his or her speaking voice) for the instructor to first read a sentence from the longer passage in a firm voice at a moderately loud dynamic level, and then to have the pupil repeat it. Together, singer and teacher listen for unwanted nasality. Ideally, the whole exercise should be recorded and played back.

When sunlight strikes raindrops in the air, they act like a prism and form a rainbow. The rainbow is a division of white light into many beautiful colors. These take the shape of a long, round arch with its path high above and its two ends apparently beyond the horizon. There is, according to legend, a boiling pot of gold at one end. People look, but no one ever finds it. When a man looks for something beyond his reach, his friends say he is looking for the pot of gold at the end of the rainbow. Throughout the centuries men have explained the rainbow in various ways. Some have accepted it as a miracle without physical explanation. To the Hebrews it was a token that there would be no more universal floods. The Greeks used to imagine that it was a sign from the gods to foretell war or heavy rain.

In today's North American society, nasality is so deeply imbedded that its presence no longer seems to disturb the casual listener. Inappropriate nasality disrupts the shapes of the resonator tract that produce the chiaroscuro timbre.

There is a drawback to techniques of singing that unduly concentrate on frontal sensation, because they encourage the substitution of nasality for the "ring" of well-balanced tone. The "ring" is provided by upper harmonic partials that result from a well-tracked vowel; nasality must not be equated with the chiaroscuro. The premise that "singing is a question of the nose" (De Reszke and his followers) hung like an albatross around the necks of several generations of French singers. Velopharyngeal closure pertains on all vowels and nonnasal consonants in Western languages, except for the aforementioned French and Portuguese nasalized vowels.

Introducing the Uses of *Strohbass*

Strohbass, in general, is not advisable practice. Strohbass is a distinctive pitch-related timbre achieved through increased laryngeal depression. (It should not be confused with vocal fry, which lacks the fullness of timbre characteristic of Strohbass.) I have repeatedly campaigned against holding the larynx in a depressed position, yet, at times, a low-voiced male can manage with authority a demanding artsong or aria, but the quick descent to one or more pitches in low register is a problem. Weakness of an important low note or two seems to preclude the performance of what otherwise could be an ideal item. On arrival at A_2, some youthful baritone timbre suddenly loses depth. This problem may crop up a minor or major third lower for the bass-baritone and the bass. It does not necessarily mean that the aria or song must be abandoned. A discreet use of *Strohbass* may come to the rescue.

Strohbass encourages momentary pharyngeal spreading. In traditional Russian liturgical and concert choirs of the recent past, a few males specialized in the Strohbass. They sang only the lowest pitches; the rest of the voice suffered from the practice. Reliance on Strohbass throughout the singing voice would be disastrous practice. However, an occasional use of Strohbass is not detrimental. A rare low note in Strohbass makes achievable literature that might otherwise be closed off to a singer.

It has been pointed out that slight laryngeal descent occurs upon complete inhalation, and that additional laryngeal lowering distorts the resonance balance by increasing low acoustic-energy levels. However, therein lies the efficacy of Strohbass as a useful device for producing the occasional elusive low note. A good maxim is, "Touch a weak low note with Strohbass, then leave the Strohbass behind."

Voce aperta (Open Timbre) and *voce chiusa* (Closed Timbre), and the Larynx as a Resonator

A premise of the early Italian School was that uniformity of timbre ought to prevail throughout the two-octave great scale. That can happen only if a singer avoids open singing in all ranges of the voice. *Voce chiusa* is dependent on the natural acoustic system wherein harmonic partials are generated by the fundamental pitch.

First, a closer look at open and closed timbres. *Voce aperta* (open voice, *voix blanche*, or white voice) upsets the chiaroscuro tone. Open singing lacks what singers and voice teachers call tonal "core" or "kernel." Vowel tracking is amiss. By contrast, voce chiusa (closed voice) is the desirably resonant voice quality of the professional singing voice. Although related phenomena, voce chiusa and voce coperta are not interchangeable terms. Voce chiusa is appropriate not only to upper-range singing but throughout the equalized scale. Popular singing styles are mostly characterized by the voce aperta timbre that classical vocalism avoids. Elite vocalism is founded on the voce chiusa principle.

To a large extent, chiusa quality depends on accurate tracking of vowels, by which process the singer retains the same concentration of acoustic energy regardless of the vowel being sung. When producing the back vowels /o/, /ʊ/, and /u/, he retains much of the "ring" present in the front vowels /i/, /ɛ/, and /e/. Vowels /i/, /ɛ/, and /e/ do not lose the "depth" of vowels /o/, /ʊ/, and /u/. The diagonal vowel sequence demonstrates vowel differentiation, but the timbre of both front and back vowels is characterized by the voce chiusa principle. In short, in the singing voice, vowels are properly "tracked" by the resonator system (see chapter 5).

A problem in low male voice may occur as the singer arrives at the passage zone (see chapter 6). If a singer does not sufficiently modify the vowel as he enters the zona di passaggio, he produces voce aperta timbre. Contrariwise, some singers who are aware of the necessity for vowel modification at the pivotal registration point indulge in excessive modification (with sudden laryngeal depression), so that the production becomes heavy. This sudden change of timbre can be avoided if the singer's larynx already lodges in a somewhat low, stabilized posture as he approaches the passage zone (see chapter 9). The ideal position is not achieved by forcibly depressing the larynx. If there is undesirable heavy action, the coperta quality that should go together with voce chiusa in upper range is turned into dark pharyngeal sound.

In the elite male voice, the lower and upper harmonic partials that produce the chiaroscuro timbre are always present. The singer who has gone through a systematic approach to vowel differentiation and voice registration will have found this center of the sound that neither thins out nor grows heavy. Yet, as has already been pointed out, because of an increase in appaggio and in distribution of acoustic energy, the larynx tends to assume a slightly lower position for pitches that lie above the singer's secondo passaggio.

Second, a word is necessary on a much-neglected topic: the contribution of laryngeal structure itself to the chiaroscuro tone. The laryngeal ventricles separate the false from the true cords, with the false vocal folds lying just above the true vocal folds. Also known as the ventricular sinuses, or as the pyriform sinuses, these adjustable spaces between the false and true folds are contributors to intralaryngeal resonance. Research indicates that the shapes of the laryngeal ventricles, which accompany the relatively low larynx, play a role in producing the chiaroscuro tone.

The role of the pyriform (piriform) sinuses has been little investigated, but studies at the Otto B. Schoepfle Vocal Arts Center, Oberlin Conservatory, show considerable alteration in the degree of openness in the pyriforms during register transition; the pyriform sinuses may well contribute to desirable resonance balance, particularly in lower range. Clearly, these phenomena (laryngeal ventricle and pyriform sinus participation) operate below the level of direct consciousness and local control.

Avoiding *voce ingolata* (Pharyngeal Timbre)

Today's opera singer has to make a large enough sound to be heard over heavy orchestration in very large performance spaces. In the thinking of many young male singers, a bigger sound is essential to a successful career. At first blush, it may seem logical that the route to a commanding voice must be the enlargement of the resonance spaces that filter the laryngeally produced tone. There are teachers of singing who add noise elements to the performer's sound in order to increase the size of the voice. Such procedures ignore the relationships among the fundamental and the first, second, and third formants.

Rearranging space of the buccal-pharyngeal tube with the aim of turning it into a fixed resonator does not enlarge the voice. Such augmentation may give the impression of increased size in the voice studio or in the practice room, but it disrupts the natural acoustics of the voice and does not add to its transport in the hall. The singer's formant is largely formed in the lower pharynx and adjoining regions, and is partially dependent on a relatively low, stabilized larynx. Conscious pharyngeal spreading reshuffles spatial relationships and adds noise to the sound.

The fullest sound a singer can make is not the product of mechanical changes in the larynx or pharynx. "It is the relationship of harmonic frequencies, not the degree of effort at the level of the larynx, that permits the 'ring' of the voice, generally described by singers and listeners as 'resonance'" (Miller, 1996, p. 272).

For the singer who suffers from voce ingolata, the best corrective move is to firmly speak the passages in question at stage-level volume. Follow by singing the segment or segments on a single pitch in the speech range, then at the primo passaggio, next at the secondo passaggio, and finally, on a pitch above the secondo passaggio pivotal point. The larynx assumes *slightly* lower positions for uppermost pitches than for those in low or middle voice (see chapter 9). The singer will most frequently enunciate without attempting pharyngeal adjustment. He will realize that no further conscious adjustment is necessary for singing than for speaking.

This additional laryngeal anchoring is in response to the compactness of head and torso and to the additional breath energy the high tessitura requires. Voce chiusa reigns throughout, with voce coperta being operative on pitches of the upper-middle and upper ranges. Voce coperta must not be confused with the manufactured, thick, heavy sound (voce ingolata) that is the consequence of the consciously spread pharynx.

Raccogliere la bocca (una bocca raccolta): Natural Communicative Expression

Dramatic veracity is diminished if the actor/singer appears to be indulging in weird facial distortions in order to retain a fixated jaw and mouth posture or to represent emotional states. An old Italian maxim suggests that the jaw and the mouth should never be falsely distended. The mouth should remain "collected" as in normal spoken communication (*raccogliere la bocca; una bocca raccolta*). This topic bridges both pedagogical and performance concerns, but because it so drastically affects performance, it is considered here among other performance reflections.

One of the most detrimental ideas prevalent in voice pedagogy is the notion that as the scale mounts, the tone moves backward and upward. "Up and back" is just as questionable as is "place it forward in the masque." One famous pedagogue advised students that singing an ascending scale is like using a bow and arrow: The farther the arrow has to go, the farther back one must pull on the bow, the bow being the pharynx and posterior portions of the head. That technique calls for spreading the fauces and widening the pharynx. I have met numerous singers who, in attempting to follow this pedagogic advice, have lost upper-range pitches and suffer from extreme weightiness in the zona di passaggio region.

The relationship of the speaking voice to the singing voice is of primary consideration. But singing is not like speaking when one leaves the speech-inflection range. Nevertheless, emphasis should be placed on the need for vowel tracking and on the resultant resonance balance that produces the chiaroscuro tone. Only when the shapes of the vocal tract are in synchronization with the subconscious formation of the vowel in the larynx will the

vowel be properly tracked. A familiar baritone aria, quoted in literature example 16.1, serves in illustration.

1. At stage-level intensity, speak the text "Bella siccome un angelo, in terra pellegrino, fresca siccome un giglio, che s'apre sul mattino," while observing the posture of lips and mouth in the hand mirror.
2. On the single note A♭₃, intone the text at the indicated rhythms. Check with the hand mirror for the same "collected mouth" position that pertained in the speech-inflection range.
3. On the single note D♭₄, intone the text in rhythm, observing by the mirror a slightly more opened mouth, which still remains within the "collected" position.
4. On the original version, sing the entire passage, noting that mouth postures resemble those observed during the preparatory exercises.

There is no "back and up," no shooting of arrows, no moving of tone into Nefertiti's hat or into a Trojan helmet! As phrases shift into and beyond the zona di passaggio, the mouth opens correspondingly. A slight increase in the degree of mouth opening occurs as the interval of the fourth is accomplished. When moving from /i/ to /ɔ/, the lips assume a more rounded position for the vowel /ɔ/ and the mouth opens a bit more, but there is no rigid "idiot" jaw posture or unchanging grin in either case. The zygomatic muscles do not drop, and the jaw is not dislocated from its sockets. Facial expression remains amiable, and the tongue undergoes essential phonetic postures. The passage is sung "with a collected mouth."

Part II

Performance Preparation and Enhancement

Chapter 17

PERFORMANCE PREPARATION
AND ENHANCEMENT

The Developmental Continuum

In writing this book, I have tried to distinguish between the needs of young artists who are engaged in the demanding professional world, and those of courageous young singers who are hoping for a performance career. In both cases, it is essential to keep in mind the developmental continuum for all of them.

The events of puberty are far more decisive for a male than for a female. If a youth has undergone puberty at age fourteen and he is now eighteen, his voice is essentially four years old. On that account, it is rare to find a young man of conservatory or university age who can compete on a technical level equal to that of a woman of the same age.

The larger the instrument, the later its maturation. Whereas the soubrette may be ready by her mid-twenties to take on professional demands, most male voices require additional time. It is traditionally and logically thought that the lyric tenor voice is the first of the male instruments to reach its fullest potential, followed in order by the baritone, the bass-baritone, and the bass.

A dilemma for the young low-voiced singer lies in conceiving of an appropriate tonal ideal for his own voice (see chapter 13). Models available to him are generally those of mature singers. He must make full use of his current voice potential but he should not force maturity. In keeping with that admonition, when choosing literature, it is wisest to concentrate on arie antiche and artsongs in languages that the less-than-mature singer can most readily manage.

My assumption throughout has been that the majority of my readers will already have made a firm commitment to pursue professionalism. There will doubtless be others who have a love for singing and who simply want to improve their vocal skills outside career goals. Learning to sing enriches life, and the nonprofessional singer will equally relish the joy that comes from learning to handle the singing voice. Everyone has a right to study singing, but objectives should be clear.

Regardless of the singer's ultimate goal, he has to master the principles of breath management, laryngeal freedom, and the phonetic nature of language (both spoken and sung). He will find information on those issues in the early chapters of this book, and he is well advised not to attempt the more strenuous parts of the recommended daily exercise regimen unless he and his teacher are certain that he is ready. The singer who wants a career is obliged to respect points of reference on the developmental continuum. Is his original vocal promise being realized? Is there evidence of a pattern of growth that encompasses voice quality, musicianship, and the art of communication? Are performance opportunities occurring at appropriate levels? Is performance a gratifying experience?

Dealing with Performance Anxiety

The best cure for performance anxiety is technical security. Of equal importance is a history of successful performance, which ought to be part of every preprofessional background. A significant advantage for the singer enrolled in academic performance-degree programs is the opportunity for regularly scheduled appearances in studio classes and departmental recitals for audiences of peers, acquaintances, and strangers. The singer who studies with a private studio teacher or coach must himself aggressively pursue modest performance outlets if, unfortunately, his mentors don't provide them. Opportunity for an emerging singer to perform publicly in preprofessional venues is essential.

As mind and body are schooled to anticipate specific maneuvers, ingrained routines remove the root causes of anxiety. Technical security remains a priority, but technique cannot be isolated from performance communication. Indeed, technique becomes the hooks on which interpretation is hung. Both artistry and technical security are established through performance.

"Performance nerves" are logical when passages of an aria or song continue to be problematic. Better to remove the item from the program than to keep it in and to worry as to whether or not it will come off. It is foolish to expect that what has not yet become a sure thing in the practice room will miraculously be corrected by the excitement that accompanies performance. Perform in public only what is secure in private. The time to "try it out" was in the performance class or for discerning listeners. A risk factor is attached to any performance, but the singer who drills difficult passages in advance establishes pathways that are predictable and repeatable. Positive performance experiences construct an arsenal of confidence.

A great deal of performance anxiety stems from lack of a complete preparation. Today's hurried singer may ingenuously consider the recital program or the opera role ready if memorization is completed by performance date. However, preparation is adequate only when the music and the text have become so ingrained that nothing short of a major distraction could break the performer's concentration.

Another cause for insecurity comes from following too closely the well-intentioned advice of a coach/accompanist, conductor, or stage director whose conceptions of the role are inappropriate to the singer's current capabilities. Not every performing artist can be expected to adhere to the phrasing so effectively used by some famous artist of the past, or to realize every dynamic subtlety a composer considered ideal for the specific voice for which he composed. A singer must not try to remake his sound in order to please a conductor or a coach who does not intimately know the singer's voice. The singer's own performance expectations, and those of his advisors, should coincide with a realistic assessment of the singer's current maturity and his musical and dramatic capabilities.

A frequent problem for the established performer is that a music critic may falsely assume that what the performer has been asked to deliver on stage represents his own artistic choice. No matter how secure or how stable his voice production, a performing artist rarely finds universal acceptance among music critics, who may have in mind a totally different tonal ideal, or a dissimilar concept of the interpretation of the role or recital material than what has been recommended to the performer. What pleases one reviewer may displease another. Nor should a singer be disturbed if a second performer—who may well have less responsibility—gets the lion's share of a reviewer's positive comments. The astute artist will soon discover that he is in competition only with his own best performance. Wise singers read reviews objectively.

Among causes for performance anxiety are unrealistic expectations on the part of the performer himself. For the singer who has heard only enthusiastic encouragement from his voice coach or agent to read the next morning the tepid critique that he was "adequate" or "competent" may come as a shock. The critic sees the performance in the context of numerous past performances; the singer is narrowly focused on his own achievement of the moment.

Perhaps the second most important antidote to performance anxiety (the first being technical security) is the removal of attention away from oneself to the process of communication. The more the singer enters into performance communication, the less concern he has for himself (see "Mastering the Art of Communication").

The Question of Relaxation

Teachers of singing look for freedom from tension or "pushing," especially as the male approaches the zona di passaggio. But the low-voiced male cannot manage the numerous tasks that lie in the zona di passaggio and in upper range through lazy singing. The answer lies in readjusting energy so as to co-ordinate breath emission and vocal-fold approximation. As a means of avoiding pressed phonation, it is sometimes recommended that the singer introduce "flow phonation" (also known as "free-flow phonation"). The student is asked to "add breath to the tone" in order to reduce any static setting of the vocal folds. Increasing the airflow as an antidote to excessive vocal-fold closure mostly generates an equally pejorative incidence of breathiness. The reader is aware that Hz pitch designations specify the number of times per second the vocal folds approximate, as in A440Hz. In healthy phonation, there is an equilibrium among the closed and open phases of the vocal folds as they react to pitch targeting. In well-supported speech, this balance indicates a nearly even airflow during both events. In pressed phonation, the length of the closed phase overbalances that of the open posture, the reverse being the case in breathy phonation. Through the use of electroglottography (EGG), the relationship of the opening and closing stages of the glottis can be measured. In normal speech, during each phonatory burst, the sound approaches a roughly 50 percent open-glottal segment and a 50 percent closed-glottal segment, graphing a kind of hat and brim effect, the hat showing the closure phase, the brim the period of glottal aperture. In breathy phonation, the glottal opening occupies more time. In pressed phonation, vocal-fold-closure becomes predominant.

As the baritone arrives at the zona di passaggio, because there is greater resistance to the exiting breath, the period of vocal-fold closure is longer, and the open phase is briefer than in speech. Some speech researchers ignore the difference between these actions in speaking and in singing. They maintain that phonation at any pitch level should retain an identical closure/open pattern. However, as has frequently been pointed out, range extension, tessitura, phrase duration, and the intensity of breath pressure (all determined by the adducting/abducting glottis) demand varying energy levels throughout the great (two-octave) scale.

It will be recalled that the baritone voce media is inclined to extend from B_3 to E_4 or $B\flat_3$ to $E\flat_4$. The bass-baritone experiences his zona di passaggio around A_3 to D_4.the bass between the regions of $A\flat_3–D\flat_4$ or $G_3–C_4$ (see chapter 1). From the first note of the passage zone to its pivotal registration point roughly a fourth above, the energy level of the airflow and the vocal-fold resistance to the exit of breath gradually increase. The closed phase lasts longer as the scale mounts. For these reasons, the transition from modal ("chest") to voce piena in testa ("full voice in head") is one of the subtlest technical tasks for the male singer.

This brings up the role that relaxation has been assigned in various voice pedagogies. Tonicity requires greater, not less, energy in the passage zone. Yet there are pedagogues who request that the singer simply "relax." A general admonition to relax lacks in specifics: What does one relax? When does one relax? How does one bring relaxation about? Relaxation is not the antonym of tension. Calling for relaxation initiates an entirely different process than that of tonicity. As Dr. Brodnitz reminded us several decades ago, if one were to totally relax he would fall to the floor. Just at the point where tonicity should be at its highest, attempting to "relax" reduces the energy level. At the same time, caution must be exercised that the low-voiced male not unduly increase vigor when singing in the zona di passaggio. As in all technical matters, the balancing out of energy levels is essential.

Female teachers who understand the physiology and the acoustics of the singing voice can teach male voices just as well as do their male colleagues. However, over a number of decades of practical encountering, it has been my experience that most female teachers do not ask their male students to energize sufficiently in upper-middle voice (the passage zone) and above, because the female voice does not require the same increase in energy in that segment of the voice that is so essential to the male instrument. As the female approaches upper-middle voice, she does not undergo as marked register alterations as do the baritone, the bass-baritone, or the bass. The reverse of that pedagogic coin is that male teachers often request greater energization from the female in upper-middle voice than is desirable.

Singing is a matter not of general relaxation but of coordinating physical, acoustic, and interpretive aspects into a dynamic equilibrium.

Marking Properly

The more stable the voice technique (the sign of a healthy production), the less need for marking. Some fine singers never mark, yet their voices remain robust. Other premier artists never sing out fully except in performance. An old theater saw says, "Sing out only when you are being paid to sing." Although I find that the latter advice is not applicable to any but the busiest performer, there are times when rehearsals and performances crowd together, or when the singer is in less than optimal physical condition, during which period marking is advisable.

A low-voiced male who is given the assignment of a dramatic Verdi role does not want to sing every musical or stage rehearsal with full voice. He must learn to mark in order to avoid the wear and tear of repetitious rehearsals, particularly those that include ensemble obligations. As a responsible cast member, he sings his entrances at normal dynamic level so as to provide clues for his colleagues, then drops back to less than full voice. For phrases that lie chiefly in the zona di passaggio and above, he fortunately can mark in an occasional falsetto (see chapter 10).

"Punktieren" is a term originating in the German theater. The occasional high note is lowered an octave. But it is unwise to transpose whole phrases that lie in the passage zone or above it to a lower octave, so that the singer is rehearsing large parts of the role in the wrong octave. This practice invites the pressing of low notes and fails to develop confidence in maintaining upper-range tessitura. A singer can, however, with impunity occasionally touch the high note an octave lower, but he must be careful not to force it.

To know how to pace a major role, the part has to be sung in its entirety. Saving the voice for the premiere is a grave mistake, because a role needs to be sung repeatedly into the voice so that the performer will know at what point technical matters need special attention. Not having sung full voice through an entire role with one's colleagues until opening night must be a nerve-wracking experience. Marking should never be used as a shelter against performance anxiety. A singer who never "sings out" in the house in advance of the performance has done himself no favor, because he has lost the benefit of accustoming his voice to the acoustic ambience. In addition, he makes dramatic and musical rapport with his colleagues difficult.

The question of how to develop stamina should be addressed. It is not a good idea to sing a dress rehearsal in full voice the day before the event. If there is more than one dress rehearsal, that which is closest to the opening night should be sung with a cautious amount of marking, or half the role should be sung with full voice at one dress, the other half at the next. The performer ought always to inform the conductor that he intends to mark at least part of an orchestral rehearsal, so that sudden reliance on less than full sound does not come about unexpectedly. The less-experienced artist ought to go over the technique of marking with his teacher or coach, making decisions in advance as to what portions to mark.

Ideally, no singer performs unless he is in good health. From time to time there are situations in which no substitute performer is available and in which the production could not go forward were the singer to cancel. One of the hardest choices a singer must make is when to cancel. The more important the engagement, the more pressure there is in reaching a decision. It is possible to sing under indisposition, but when the larynx itself is the source the singer must cancel ("The Daily Regimen and Healthy Vocalism"). Marking can be an occasional aid for the healthy voice, and a reliable mode for easing the weary or suffering voice, but it must never become customary.

Prevocal Warm-Up Activity

Some singers engage in long vocal warm-ups. They think the voice will be ready only after a long period of preparatory vocalizing. In trying to warm up the voice, they tire it. They sing the bloom off the voice before the curtain goes up. By contrast, the artist who does his vocal warm-up during act 1 does himself, his colleagues, and his audience a disservice. Both situations can be avoided through physical actions that take place immediately before engaging in strenuous vocalism.

The vocal warm-up itself should not be the sole awakening process for musculatures involved in singing. Elite singing can be partially readied by prior physical groundwork. It makes little sense for a singer to plunge into strenuous vocalises and to sing challenging arias without first awakening the muscle groups implicated in intense tasks. An athlete uses physical warm-ups before heavy-duty involvement, and the serious vocalist will do likewise. It is false to assume that the muscles on which vocalization rely are at the ready without some preparation.

General physical alertness undergirds performance readiness. Certain muscle groups are more directly involved in high levels of vocal fitness than are others. Any muscle that establishes stance and body balance is part of the singing instrument. Included among them:

1. nuchal muscles (muscles of the back of the neck) that help achieve the noble position and lend external support to the larynx.
2. sternocleidomastoids, scaleni, capitis and trapezius muscles, which determine axial posture.
3. muscles of the pectoral and sternum regions, which determine the position of the ribcage.
4. anterior and lateral muscles of the abdominal region, which establish favorable conditions for the appoggio.
5. all muscles that maintain a unity of the torso, and which extend from the pelvis/ buttocks/ hip foundation to the occipital region of the skull (see chapter 9).

The most effective use of time and energy is to devise specific body-mapping exercises that involve muscle groups activated in singing. Taken altogether, these prephonatory, nonsinging exercises require approximately twenty to twenty-five minutes. If possible, in an academic setting, I meet the new studio members first as a group to go over the physical exercises, so that I do not lose lesson time. If not, we must use precious studio time to review them. The exercises should be executed in an established order (relaxing a moment or two between each series). Each should be implemented several times.

EXERCISE 17.1. SIDEWAYS HIP
MOVEMENT, WITH ARMS OVER
THE HEAD

Upon silent inhalation, raise the arms high over the head, making certain that the spine is as straight as possible. Move the hips side-to-side, while keeping the sternum facing forward.

EXERCISE 17.2. BODY DROP, SILENT EXHALATION, AND SILENT INHALATION

Upon silent exhalation, drop the hands as near the floor as possible; hang the head to its lowest position. Then inhale silently and bring the body upward, while raising the arms over the head.

EXERCISE 17.3. SIDEWAYS STERNOCLEIDOMASTOIDAL RESISTANCE

While keeping the sternum positioned straight forward, move the head gently to the left, until resistance is felt at the sternocleidomastoid muscle. Hold the contact position for five seconds. Use the same action by moving the head to the right, feeling similar sternocleidomastoid resistance.

EXERCISE 17.4. "FLYING"

Reestablish the noble axial posture. Fully extend the hands and arms out to the sides of the torso and move the arms in small, circular patterns. Reverse the direction of circular movements.

EXERCISE 17.5. "WIND-MILLING"

Keeping the sternum directly forward, swing the right arm leftward across the torso, then the left arm rightward. Keep it going.

EXERCISE 17.6. HANDS ON HIPS; ALTERNATE SIDEWAYS HIP MOVEMENT

Place a hand on each hip and move the hips sideways, both left and right, sternum facing forward, while maintaining a stable torso.

EXERCISE 17.7. BODY BEND

Hands on hips, lean backward as far as comfortable, pelvis thrust forward, with quiet deep inhalation. Return to an axial standing posture on exhalation.

EXERCISE 17.8. "LEONARDO DA VINCI" STRETCH

This maneuver assumes the axial posture depicted in Leonardo da Vinci's famous male-body study. Standing erect with the feet slightly apart, raise the arms over the head as high as possible; then assume arm positions midway between elevated and horizontal. Now lower the arms to a horizontal position. Next, assume a still lower position midway between horizontal and perpendicular. Conclude with the arms hanging loosely relaxed at the sides.

EXERCISE 17.9. SIT-UPS OR BODY CRUNCHES

Begin with several slowly executed sit-ups or body crunches. Over time, increase the number.

EXERCISE 17.10. HIP MOVEMENT IN SEATED POSITION

While seated, with the torso axial, slowly turn the hips to the left, then to the right.

EXERCISE 17.11. PUSHUPS

Slowly do a series of pushups, increasing the number over time.

It is understood that individual physical conditions may require caution in using each of the exercises suggested. But it should be recognized, as many premier performers have noted, that the entire body is involved in singing. Some singers practice body-conditioning systems that include drills in mental quietude. Both action and tranquility can be of value in prevoice warm-ups.

Early Career Preparation and Pursuit

Suppose, for a moment, that you are a seventeen-year-old baritone and that you have had good choral experiences in high school, have sung leads in school musicals, have consistently placed first or second in singing contests in your state, have been a member of all-state chorus, and have been encouraged by persons in your community to pursue a professional singing career. The conservatories or schools of music to which you are applying may have asked you to write a brief "career goal" essay. Many such short essays read something like, "I want to develop my voice so I will be able to sing at the

Metropolitan Opera and at internationally famous opera houses." What a great goal! How realistic is it, and on what factors does its realization depend?

Statistically, the number of North American conservatory performance-major graduates who end up in professional singing careers is relatively small. Most with professional ambitions were admitted to major conservatories and schools of music on promise shown when auditioning. What determines the difference between those who succeed in performance careers and those who do not? Requirements often seem elusive, yet are identifiable.

A major singing career requires high-level musicianship, a skill that is acquirable by most persons who have been drawn to a life in music. Early musical skills can contribute to superior musicianship but do not ensure a career. Most potential professional male singers discover only in their mid-teens that they have an instrument that sets them apart from others. They generally have much catching up to do. But catch up they must.

Long gone are the days of the great singing voice that could make a career despite its possessor's inability to rapidly read and learn music. A great instrument attached to an unmusical, untrained individual has no professional value. The stronger the musical background, the faster will be the rate of professional progress. Although he may not be able to ace his music theory exams, the superior singer/musician knows how to make a vocal line come alive, and he understands how to direct and shape a phrase. He also must comprehend the underlying support that harmonic language gives to melodic excursion. Despite the importance of a musicianly background, the chief prerequisite remains the singer's ability to conceive a beautiful tonal ideal that is in accordance with his native instrument. In the end, the capacity to conceive of and to achieve beautiful timbre is the highest form of musicianship to which any performer can aspire (see chapter 13).

How often does a great voice arrive at any studio door complete with a tonal ideal and a secure technique? For practical purposes, never! The vocal instrument may be a hidden Stradivarius, but just as a great violin must be in the hands of someone who knows how to play it, so the great singing voice demands a trained executor—the well-schooled singer. In past eras, many of a professional singer's waking hours were devoted to skills that would allow the fullest realization of his voice potential. Today's student is in a great hurry. He seldom has the luxury of total immersion in professional preparation. Despite that, he can move more quickly forward if he is willing to take on the daily task of building a stable voice technique. In doing so, the singer dare not waste time in experimenting with whatever may be the most current voice fad but, rather, takes advantage of verifiable information on the functional aspects of the singing voice. He may need to find a teacher who can communicate them to him.

An artistic temperament is not always immediately apparent, but it can be nurtured and developed. The creative spirit remains as indefinable as the human psyche. Beautiful sounds not connected to a creative personality are of limited value. However, all too often a voice coach or a teacher of singing writes off a young singer because he seems to lack imagination. His perceived inability to communicate also can be obscured by technical considerations and performance anxieties (see "Mastering the Art of Communication"). An essential in the building of a successful career is the singer's own objectivity. It is all well and good for the teacher of an unusually gifted student to encourage him and lead him to believe that he is headed for stardom—he will need a strong ego and a firm belief in himself—but many a singer has fallen by the wayside because of a lack of objective self-examination. Opera departments at major schools of music offer first-rate preprofessional training for talented students, but in the process tend to breed singers who are overly expectant regarding career opportunities. Unless objectivity remains a pillar of the total professional package, the singer will have a difficult road ahead.

Most singers assume that the most important factor in building a career is voice talent. They are mistaken. It is not always the most beautiful voice that is the most successful one. There are many beautiful voices. How voice talent is nurtured makes the difference. Serious study is prerequisite number one. Entering and winning competitions appropriate to one's level, exploring foundation grants, participating in nationally known summer performance programs, or finding a committed sponsor are routes that may open professional doors. A number of information sources are available to today's aspiring singer, including magazines devoted to the classical performer, the Internet, and authors who offer career advice. Most schools of music list performance opportunities, and a number offer courses in career management.

Music is big industry, and a successful singer needs to explore paths that facilitate entrance into the business of singing. Young singers sometimes idealistically expect to be "discovered." They assume that agents are waiting to invest in a singer's career. Any male who is serious about building a career must himself search out ways to penetrate the singing industry. Career building is a tall ladder with many steps, and the upward climb is an arduous one. Almost without exception, it is a long haul.

Is the aspirant disposed to give building a career the time and the effort it requires? Will he be willing to accept lesser niches in the musical world if the big goal remains elusive? The young baritone who writes his application essay and comes for his initial studio interview may know only of the Met as an ultimate goal. If he is to retain his equilibrium and objectivity (indeed, his sanity), he must become aware of the existence of diverse possibilities for performance and service. Will he find satisfaction in the love of performance regardless of its location and its level? At some point, he must ask himself if all that will be required of him is worth it. Only if his commitment is so strong that he is willing to ride with the ups and downs, the successes and the failures, should he give his life over to a career objective.

Along the way there must be favorable indications from persons who understand what it takes to build a career. A singer should become familiar with the circuitous routes by which other performers have arrived. If, having faced the realities, he is willing to try his hand, the decision must go forward with an all-consuming drive. Career rewards can be great, but the expenditures in time, money, energy, and patience can be demanding. Learning to sing is both pleasurable and challenging. There are few major careers that have not encountered some valleys and mountaintops. A committed singer must learn to maintain an even compass as he steers his way over the bumpy terrain of career building.

Mastering the Art of Communication

Preprofessional and professional competition adjudication panels generally include one or more prominent teachers of singing, one or two celebrated performing artists, a conductor, a coach/accompanist, a stage director, and perhaps a management representative. Some consist entirely of voice teachers and artists of note. Although all judges share an overall understanding of the prerequisites for career pursuit, each judge brings a particular set of credentials to bear. Yet seasoned adjudicators look for a package that includes a unique singing quality, musicianly intelligence, linguistic accuracy, assured physical presence, and, above all, the ability to communicate. Wise judges take into consideration the contest level and the ages of the contestants.

An eighteen-year-old man auditioning for a conservatory or school of music has to impress the voice faculty committee with considerable voice potential and musical sensitivity, but seldom can be expected to reveal accomplished technical control and stylistic finesse. It is inappropriate for an auditioning committee to refuse degree-program entrance to a young male who shows good voice material but has not yet "learned to say something when he sings." He probably is petrified at having to sing his first audition in a language he has mostly learned by rote, and in a style with which he has had little association. His attention is focused on the technical things his teacher has taught him. Undergraduate degree-program entrance auditions should not be searches for finished products but be based on potential. Most young men are farther along in some one aspect than in others. Many successful professional singers recall having been refused entrance to undergraduate performance programs at more than one major school of music. Early judgments are by no means final.

How should the young singer prepare for auditions? He must become convinced that there is no dichotomy between technique and interpretation. Technical maneuvers should become communicative expressions. He ought never to sing without filling his practice room with an imaginary audience. Each practice session is a performance. His own ears are a part of that audience.

In the song literature, the singer uses words that he himself did not write and music he did not compose. Although he is the recreator, not the creator, he needs to bring a sense of spontaneity to both words and music. The procedures for doing this are as teachable and as learnable as is technique.

It begins with the text. The singer should read the text of the song or aria aloud, being aware of who the character is and in what circumstances the character is entangled. It is essential to know the meaning of every word, not just the overall dramatic situation. He should inflect the spoken line of poetry or prose in several ways and at several dynamic levels; then intone a few verses of the text as it is rhythmically constructed, on a single pitch in a comfortable range. Finally, he should sing the phrase as written. Neighboring phrases are gradually added and the same procedure is followed.

Of major importance for the skilled artist is the capacity to visualize the drama and to imagine the emotion that underlies it. This imagery must be as sharp as reality. If possible, this inner visualization should be in color. How is the fisher maiden dressed? What color is her hair? Is she wearing a head covering? How old is she? What size is her boat? The interpreter knows what a gathering storm feels like, the wonderment of being alone in the forest, the joy of companionship, the pain of loss. The situation with its persons and objects are so real that he could reach out and touch them.

The experienced singer will mentally add a text between lines of the drama, using what is on the printed page as the point of departure for renewing each accumulating image. A sense of immediacy is the ultimate aim. A part of the mind acts as a technical monitor, especially in vocally challenging moments, but the imagination and the spirit of communication flow uninterruptedly.

It takes practice to develop conscious awareness of this creative process. The young baritone freshman who stands before the audition committee and sings his favorite song (yes, it's "The Vagabond" again!) wants to make sure that he has his climactic notes properly in order; in the process, he may overlook the joy of the youthful wanderer. His "Come away, Death" remains an exercise in vocalization. The profundity of the text seems to have escaped him. Have him delve into the dramatic situation of both songs. Stage the song or aria. Then drop the stage movements while retaining the dramatic visualization of the text.

An experienced teacher learns to deal with the kind of male personality that finds it difficult to express strong emotion. The student may at first be hesitant, because he feels insincere in trying to portray emotions he has never personally experienced. Some young male singers are afraid to be expressive for fear of pretending emotions they do not honestly feel. It must be pointed out that art is not reality. It is not necessary to *experience* the emotional states of burning love, strong hatred, scheming intrigue, or the triumph of revenge. It is indispensable to learn how to *portray* those emotions. He must learn that the artist does not undergo all the pain, rejection, nostalgia, hope, joy, and love that the texts express. Art is the transformation of reality, not reality itself.

A second kind of personality wants to throw himself into the emotion to the extent that he becomes so involved that continuing to sing becomes problematic. The singer's job is not to engage in self-indulgent emotional baths in public but to reenact sentiment. One could not experience the rage that Verdi's Ford portrays and sing at the same time. When Caleb calls for the raging flames to arise, he does not experience the actual excitement of battle; the seasoned baritone learns how to represent rage, not to actually undergo it. In all the dramatic situations he represents, a communicative performer must know which of his facial expressions match the drama. He should be acquainted with them by having observed himself beforehand in the mirror or on videotape.

No matter how small the room or performance hall, it has these dimensions—front, left, and right. The recitalist must place fantasy audience members in all parts of the hall (whether it is crowded or empty), occasionally directly addressing someone in each area. As the mood or scene changes, so do his glance and the center of his communication, but never in some predictable sequence. In concert, the singer must not focus on some one spot in the hall, located above the heads of his audience. (Forget the legendary clock at center balcony!) He needs to establish eye contact with members of his audience, and he must not sing through them or above them, except in rare introspective moments. A singer alone on the stage extends the stage outward to include everyone. Each lied, each mélodie, each artsong is a miniature drama to be portrayed within recital conventions.

In opera, the singer is assisted by colleagues to whom he can relate, as well as by lights, costumes, and the buoying effect of the orchestra. Alone on the recital stage, in his inward vision he must mentally surround himself with those supports. Although not physically present, they are with him in his imagination.

Many young males have been schooled by surrounding society to keep their feelings under wraps; they are conditioned to feel that emotional display is not masculine. The truly artistic personality learns to portray both masculine and feminine feelings, sometimes within the same composition. A skillful interpreter loses none of his masculinity in so doing. It may require time for the baritone, bass-baritone, or bass to hold onto his emerging technique and at the same time allow his imagination to come to the fore. He must become convinced that the only reason for technical prowess is to master musical and interpretative expression.

Daily Regimen and Healthy Vocalism

No matter how stable his technique or how well he performs the standard literature, every singer should tailor a short daily regimen selected from separate areas of technical concentration. A singer should pull together a daily protocol that covers items from the major areas that have been identified in this manual. The daily regimen will keep the singer on track and let him know the condition of his voice.

Not every day is an equal day in the life of a singer. Physical and emotional upsets directly challenge the evenness of production. One may feel "out of voice" but unable to locate a specific cause. Through adherence to the daily protocol, the singer will know where his instrument stands on any particular day. There are times when the warm-up period leading to performance requires attention to specific aspects of technique.

On a concert day, it is foolhardy to wait to discover how one's voice feels until shortly before the hour of performance. Early in the day, a judicious singer goes through a reduced protocol, consisting of a limited number of onsets, resonance balancing vocalises, and velocity patterns. He should avoid the more strenuous sostenuto and vowel modification exercises on a performance day, or touch only a few of them. Then, shortly before the public appearance, several minutes given over to a quick run of favorite exercises throughout the entire voice, provides assurance that "everything is there."

It is possible to sing when ill, but it must be done advisedly. One can sing under a number of adverse circumstances—even with upper respiratory difficulties. But if the disturbance is in the larynx, performance is out of the question. If the singer continues to limp along, performance by performance, several days of complete abstinence from phonation may prove the answer.

The question as to how long voice rest should be continued depends, of course, on the nature and seriousness of the affliction. If a singer has laryngitis, he should refrain from singing, and even from speaking for several days, resorting to written communication. This period of silence should be as brief as possible. Above all, the ill singer should not resort to whispering at a volume that is loud enough to be heard in normal conversation. If incapacitated for more than a week, or ten days at the most, he should consult a laryngologist (or voice wellness clinician) who has had experience in dealing with the professional singing voice. Prolonged voice rest should be undertaken only with the advice of an ENT or a professional voice-user specialist.

The daily protocol should always be preceded by a brief nonvocal warm-up period (see "Prevocal Warm-Up Activity"). A professional performer with back-to-back commitments ought to decide on a concise protocol, in which technical bases are briefly touched without undue wear and tear on the instrument. Running through large sections of the role or the recital before the performance is ill advised. Checking tempi with the accompanist, if at all necessary, should be limited to that enterprise.

An active performer may be required to sing Handel, Mozart, Verdi, and Puccini within a short time span. He must be physically and mentally ready for whatever style he is called on to deliver. Few indeed are the artists who can limit their performances to specific roles or to a narrow choice of composers. If he has been concentrating on recital material, the singer must not neglect his operatic literature. If, for example, he is occupied with *Winterreise* or *Dichterliebe,* he must not overlook Mozart and Massenet. An outstanding baritone artist said in an interview that, following a tour of lieder recitals, he found it took a period of singing Rossini to bring him back to his full vocal potential. Had he done his daily protocol of selections from the range of technical exercises during the lieder tour, that most probably would not have been the case.

A number of fine low-voiced male performers are also teachers of singing. In addition to being responsible for the welfare of talented students, they must maintain their own flourishing careers. If the artist/teacher has recital or stage engagements, he should as much as possible try to put his teaching duties on temporary hold. No singer has the concentration and energy it takes to perform a substantial opera role or a strenuous recital and to simultaneously carry on all of his normal teaching duties.

Useful Passages from the Literature

In addition to select vocalises from the daily protocol, short passages from the literature ought to be interspersed or sung at the close of the vocal warm-up session. The following lists contain examples from which mature singers may wish to select additional warm-up phrases. They serve a different purpose from the earlier listings for less advanced singers.

For the Baritone

"Grosser Herr und starker König," *Weihnachtsoratorium,* J. S. Bach

"Non più andrai," *Le nozze di Figaro,* Mozart

"Aprite un po' quegli occhi," *Le nozze di Figaro,* Mozart

"Se vuol ballare," *Le nozze di Figaro,* Mozart

"Avant de quitter," *Faust,* Gounod

"Di Provenza il mar," *La traviata,* Verdi

For the Bass-Baritone

"Madamina," *Don Giovanni,* Mozart

"Dormirò sol nel manto mio regal," *Don Carlo,* Verdi

"Quand la flamme de l'amour," *La jolie fille de Perth,* Bizet

"Épouse quelque brave fille," *Manon,* Massenet

"Hat man nicht auch Gold daneben," *Fidelio,* Beethoven

"Vi ravviso," *La sonnambula,* Bellini

For the Bass

"In diesen heil'gen Hallen," *Die Zauberflöte,* Mozart

"Si la rigeur," *La Juive,* Halévy

"Als Büblein klein," *Die lustigen Weiber von Windsor,* Nicolai

"Il lacerato spirito," *Simon Boccanegra,* Verdi

"Infelice! e tu credevi," *Ernani,* Verdi

Chapter 18

EARLY REPERTOIRE SUGGESTIONS

For most North American male singers of university or conservatory age, it is almost always most rewarding to begin voice study with literature in the native language, which generally is English. Possibilities seem endless, but should include some of the basic literature listed here.

A Few Less-Demanding Items for Baritone

English-language

Handel

"Leave Me, Loathsome Light"

"Thanks Be to Thee, Lord God of Hosts"

"Vouchsafe, O Lord"

Purcell

"I Attempt from Love's Sickness to Fly"

"Music for Awhile"

Barber

"With Rue My Heart Is Laden"

Bowles

"Cabin," *Mountain Ballads*

Britten

"Salley Gardens," *Folksongs of the British Isles*

"The Ash Grove"

"O Waly, Waly"

Chanler

"The Lamb"

Copland

"'Tis the Gift to Be Simple," *Old American Songs*

Duke

"Loveliest of Trees"

Ives

"Shall We Gather at the River"

"Two Little Flowers"

"Evening"

Because of the favorability of the Italian language for singing, every young baritone should early encounter a number of songs (arie antiche) in Italian. The following list contains items readily available in commercial collections.

Italian-language

Caccini

"Amarilli, mia bella"

Bononcini

"La speranza i cori affida"

"Per la gloria d'adorarvi"

Caldara

"Alma del core"

"Come raggio di sol"

Durante

"Danza, danza, fanciulla gentile"

Giordani (Giordanello)

"Caro mio ben"

Gluck

"O del mio dolce ardor"

Marcello

"Il mio bel foco"

Monteverdi

"Lasciatemi morire!"

Porpora

"Come la luce è tremola"

A. Scarlatti

"Già il sole dal Gange"

"Sebben, crudele"

"O cessate di piagarmi"

Stradella

"Pietà, Signore!"

Torelli

"To lo sai"

The proliferation of phonetic sounds in the French language may make it wise to delay early assignments for the native English-language speaker. However, for the singer who has some acquaintance with the rules of French pronunciation, a few excellent sources are listed here.

French-language

Lulli

"Bois épais"

Fauré

"Lydia"

"Adieu"

"Chanson d'amour"

Hahn

"Offrande"

"Si mes vers"

Because the heart of the artsong literature lies in the lied, a singer should begin exploring German-language sources as early as possible.

German-language

J. S. Bach

"Komm, süsser Tod"

"Bist du bei mir"

"Betrachte meine Seel'"

Schubert

"An die Musik"

"Das Wandern"

"Wohin?"

"Der Wanderer"

Beethoven

"Ich liebe dich"

Schumann

"Widmung"

"Du bist wie eine Blume"

"Der Nussbaum"

"Die beide Grenadiere"

Brahms

"Der Gang zum Liebchen"

"Vergebliches Ständchen"

"In stiller Nacht"

"Mein Mädel hat einen rosen Mund"

A Few Less-Demanding Items for Bass-Baritone and Bass

English-language

Purcell

"I Attempt from Love's Sickness to Fly"

"Music For Awhile"

"Arise, Ye Subterranean Winds"

Handel

"Leave Me, Loathsome Light"

"Thanks Be to Thee"

Carpenter

"May, the Maiden"

"To One Unknown"

Rorem

"Cherry Ripe"

"Upon Julia's Clothes"

Italian-language

Monteverdi

"Lasciatemi morire!"

Gluck

"O del mio dolce ardor"

Caldara

"Come raggio di sol"

Marcello

"Il mio bel foco"

Durante

"Vergin, tutto amor"

Legrenzi

"Che fiero costume"

Beethoven

"In questa tomba oscura"

French-language

Lulli

"Bois épais"

Fauré

"Lydia"

"Adieu"

Poulenc (from *Le bestiaire*)

"Le dromadaire"

"La chêvre du Thibet"

"La sauterelle"

"Le dauphin"

"La carpe"

Hahn

"Offrande"

"Si mes vers"

German-language

Beethoven

"Aus Goethes Faust"

"Bitten"

"Die Liebe des Nächsten"

"Vom Tode"

"Gottes Macht und Vorsehung"

Schubert

"Das Fischermädchen"

"Fischerweise"

Schumann

Vier Husarenlieder

"Der Husar, trara!"

"Der leidige Frieden"

"Den grünen Zeigern"

"Da liegt der Feinde gestreckte Schar"

Chapter 19

CHOOSING AUDITION MATERIAL

Judges would rather hear a modest aria sung with finesse and skill than watch and listen to a singer fight his way through a heavier selection. Lyric voices ought not to present dramatic arias that contain high demands on stamina, sustained passaggio work, and dramatic dynamics. Better by far that the young baritone present "Aprite un po'" rather than "Cortigiani." Singers tell their teachers, "But it's the big voices that win the competitions." On the contrary, it is the singer who selects appropriate material, who handles it well, and who presents it with conviction who is chosen.

For an audition, it is unwise to choose a lengthy aria, unless the item has been specifically requested. Be certain to sing your best item first. Do not save it for another round (which may never come). Most judges make up their minds about talent and potential during the first thirty to sixty seconds of singing. Generally, the singer will be permitted to choose his own first aria; the adjudicators may then select one or two others. At callbacks, the singer is usually asked for something other than his first-round choice. Because contrasting material will allow the judges to evaluate vocal prowess more fully, something bravura and something of a cavatina nature should be among the available choices.

Contest rules are often generous with regard to lower age limits, in the eternal hope that some great young instrument may make an early appearance. Some singers believe they should enter every contest that does not specifically exclude them on the basis of age. Many singers in their late teens or early twenties lack the maturity of voice for the competition they enter. It doesn't matter that the notes of an aria are all there and that the timbre is agreeable. What matters is the appropriateness of the size and weight of the voice for the expectations of that specific competition. No matter how well a twenty-one-year-old baritone handles a standard aria, when competing with well-trained twenty-eight-year-olds, it is improbable that he will place ahead of them. (Exceptions are rare.) A wise choice is for the young baritone, bass-baritone, or bass to audition for summer programs where he may first serve as a member of the chorus, be assigned small roles, or be cast as a cover for a major role (see chapter 17).

His voice mentor must help the singer to decide when to audition, for which contests, and what items to use. Many young artist competitions and comparable foundation-supported auditions call for five arias in several languages. The arias should be so secure that they are performable on "automatic pilot." One famous international coach maintained that five arias should be so ingrained that "you could fall out of bed in the morning, land on your head, stand up, and sing them." This is not good literal advice, but it is indicative of how thoroughly the audition material ought to be assimilated. Yet, no matter how long the association with an aria, it must have the spark of immediacy about it when it is performed.

Appendix 1

A SAMPLING OF A FEW GREAT BARITONES, BASS-BARITONES, AND BASSES OF THE PAST AND PRESENT WHO SERVE AS GOOD MODELS

Until the advent of the gramophone, a documentation of historic vocalism depended on contemporaneous reviews and comments. With the advent of the recording industry, acquaintance with the technical and artistic level of great singers of the past is possible. To present a complete list of worthy singers, past and present, would take a separate volume. I have restricted myself to a narrow selection of low-voiced male singers who have been recorded, and have served, or continue to serve, as fine exemplars for baritones, bass-baritones, and basses. It must be understood that it excludes many other fine artists. Some prominent names have been omitted because they are so artistically distinctive that I do not think they serve as appropriate models. (The same criterion would keep me from suggesting that Enrico Caruso should be the model for most tenors!) Alas, it is also the case that some artists of lengthy career experiences were at their best in earlier decades, and I hesitate to include them as current models.

Baritones

Thomas Allen

Carlos Alvarez

Gabriel Bacquier

Mario Basiola

Ettore Bastianini

Richard Bonelli

Renato Bruson

Renato Capecchi

Piero Cappuccilli

Vladimir Chernov

Giuseppe De Luca

Pablo Elvira

Tito Gobbi

Igor Gorin

Frank Guarrera

Thomas Hampson

Mack Harrell

Dmitri Hvorostovsky

Cornell MacNeil

Robert Merrill

Josef Metternich

Sherrill Milnes

Juan Pons

Hermann Prey

Louis Quilico

Titta Ruffo

Antonio Scotti

Riccardo Stracciari

Giuseppe Taddei

Carlo Tagliabue

John Charles Thomas

Lawrence Tibbett

Leonard Warren

Lawrence Winters

Bass-Baritones and Basses

Theo Adam, bass-baritone

Walter Berry, bass-baritone/bass

Kurt Böhme, bass

Kim Borg, bass-baritone

Fyodor Chaliapin [Shalyapin], bass

Boris Christoff, bass

Justino Díaz, bass

Ezio Flagello, bass

Nicolai Ghiaurov, bass

Donald Gramm, bass-baritone

Hans Hotter, bass-baritone

Alexander Kipnis, bass

Erich Kunz, bass-baritone

Nicola Rossi-Lemeni, bass-baritone

Robert Lloyd, bass

John Macurdy, bass

James Morris, bass-baritone

René Pape, bass

Ezio Pinza, bass

Pol Plançon, bass

Thomas Quasthoff, bass-baritone

Ruggero Raimondi, bass-baritone/bass

Samuel Ramey, bass-baritone/bass

John Relyea, bass-baritone

Cesare Siepi, bass

Italo Tajo, bass-baritone/bass

Martti Talvela, bass

Bryn Terfel, bass-baritone

Giorgio Tozzi, bass-baritone/bass

José Van Dam, bass-baritone

William Warfield, bass-baritone

Appendix 2

WHAT SHOULD THE WELL-EQUIPPED TEACHER KNOW?

A singer about to enter a new studio should ask an important question: "What does this teacher of singing know?" The vast amount of information on the singing voice assembled over the centuries is daunting. No one can lay claim to a comprehensive knowledge of all of it, but it is essential that a teacher be aware of the existence of basic historic and current information as to how the vocal instrument behaves.

Today's teachers are mostly recruited from one of two environments: (1) retired professional singers who have had successful careers, and (2) candidates who have completed university school-of-music doctoral performance programs. In the first instance, the teacher's reputation as a successful performer may be the chief, even at times sole, credential. Inasmuch as personal discovery is not without difficulty transferable to another individual, the communication of technical precepts has to be something more than subjective and descriptive. It is for this reason that only a few great singing artists have achieved high rates of success in the pedagogy field.

It should be said at once that the know-how that comes from having experienced a singing career is irreplaceable. The artist who night after night and year after year has communicated his or her artistry to a waiting public possesses a kind of wisdom that can never be duplicated by the occasional performer. Such information, however, may be limited with regard to the essentials of voice-building. For that reason, master classes with most famous singers generally show great strength in matters of interpretation and communication but disclose little help in the solution of technical concerns. No matter how personably the master classes and lessons may be presented, seldom is enduring substance gained.

In the second instance, the teacher most probably entered a conservatory or school of music as a voice performance major with every hope of success in pursuing a professional career. Despite recognition as a singer of merit, he or she may have seen the wisdom of accumulating advanced credentials—

the master's, the artist diploma, or the doctor of musical arts (D.M.A.) degrees. During the course of training, this person will have encountered pedagogy courses and probably have taught "secondary" (nonmajor) voice students, as part of graduate fellowships. He or she was probably called on to teach both males and females. Have the artist teacher and the new D.M.A. assembled the know-how each will need to deal with a wide range of voice issues?

There is a basic historic literature that contains essential knowledge. Much of it is gathered in treatises and books on the art of singing. Every discipline has such a solid body of literature, and it is as incumbent on the person who chooses the voice-teaching field to be familiar with those critical sources as it is for the professional of any occupation to know those of his or her field. Such is the minimal requirement. By reading the pedagogy literature, he or she becomes aware of which books are most frequently cited in references and bibliographies. (Many titles are included in the select bibliography.) The acquisition of teaching tools is a gradual process. It cannot be accomplished immediately. By reading the pedagogic literature, and by listening to examples of great singing in live and recorded performances, a teacher broadens his pedagogic horizons.

A teacher should invest in a pedagogy library. It is as essential to have such materials as to possess music scores. A student who sees no reference books in his teacher's studio (and no music scores) should be on guard. He would not frequent a law office devoid of reference volumes. Such an omission may well indicate that the teacher's knowledge is limited to what he or she has personally encountered.

North American pedagogy made great strides in the second half of the twentieth century and continues to do so in the twenty-first. For decades, it was customary for singers in Europe to enter the teaching profession in their declining years, after having established themselves as foremost opera singers. One went from having found the answers to one's own voice over several decades to immediately attempting to place personal sensations on someone else. That recruitment policy has altered considerably in the last several decades.

Every person who teaches singers ought to have a practical knowledge of the workings of the laryngeal and breath-management mechanisms. This should be precise, not superficial, information. A smattering of knowledge can be as dangerous as no information. One does not have to invent physiology and acoustics. They are exact sciences, and they have been precisely defined. Why not become acquainted with them as they pertain to the voice? Knowing the names of muscles is of little importance, but an awareness of their coordination in phonation and breath-management is vital. Understanding the source of vocal sound and its acoustic enrichment is indispensable. Such information can be gained within a year or two at most. Essential functional knowledge is readily available, but acquiring it calls for motivation, study, and patience.

As earlier mentioned, interpreting spectral analysis of the singing voice is an easily learned skill. It serves as an accessory tool in assisting the singer and his teacher to see as well as to hear the differences that he can make in his voice timbres. The concept of an ideal singing sound becomes clearer. How naïve was the artist teacher who used to boast in master classes that she had never read a book on singing or on sex but had not done badly in either. Success with that kind of voice teaching is bound to be hit or miss. Such a teacher may prove to be an excellent literature coach, but a "voice-building" technician for all voice types, hardly!

Fortunately, the last half-century has moved the general level of voice pedagogy into more reliable territory. That is opportune, because today's student is not interested in the idiosyncratic notions of his instructor or in career reminiscences, but is looking for solid assistance in furthering his own career. The ethical teacher will recognize the need to have the most complete musical, interpretive, and technical equipage possible.

Appendix 3

IPA SYMBOLS FOR SOME SUNG VOWELS, WITH MODEL WORDS

	Symbol	English	French	German	Italian
front (lateral)	/i/	keen	lis	Liebe	prima
	/I/	thin		mit	
	/e/	chaos	été	Leben	pena
	/ɛ/	bet	neige, père	Bett, Gäste	tempo
	/a/	bat	parle		
back (rounded)	/ɑ/	father	âge	Stadt	camera
	/ɔ/	all	mort	Sonne	morto
	/o/	no	pauvre	Sohn	non
	/U/	look		Mutter	
	/u/	fool	ou	Mut	uso
	/ə/	ahead	demain	getan	
	/y/		une	Müde	
	/Y/			Glück	
	/œ/		heure	Köpfe	
	/ø/		peu	schön	

181

Appendix 4

THE TEN COMMANDMENTS OF VOICE PEDAGOGY (DIAGNOSING AND PRESCRIBING)

I take the liberty of expressing some personal thoughts in this final appendix. It has been my privilege to have encountered fine preprofessional and professional singers. Many have gone on to prominent careers. What primary principles characterize all of them?

One must be equally a musician and a singer. An emerging singer quickly realizes that the only reason for having technical means is to convey musicianly and dramatic communication. Only if he acquires the technical skills of his instrument will he be able to communicate to a listening public.

During a long teaching career, much of it in public forums, it has given me personal joy to share pedagogic ideas with enthusiastic colleagues and performers as we joined together in the search for a stable voice pedagogy. Yet over the years there has been the occasional Doubting Thomas who feared that precise knowledge about the voice as an instrument would hinder artistry. Some have remained unconvinced that subjective language might be augmented by factual specificity. One teacher felt the need to set me straight by saying that, even after a week of lectures and teaching demonstrations, I had failed to mention "the banana in the throat." Another wondered why I had not explained how to open the frontal sinuses, while yet a third asked me to manually feel how he "opened his throat."

Not long ago, at the close of a weekly course for teachers and singers evenly divided between voice technique and performance communication, I received this written question: "You seem to build a lot of your teaching on knowing how the instrument works. Why don't you skip all of that sort of thing and just go directly to building a person's musical performance, which you eventually do anyway?" In addition to the fact that much of my time is spent in attempting to convey the stylistic and musicianly aspects of performance, the answer to that comment is that musicianship requires skills placed at the disposal of the artistic imagination. Technique and artistry are equally essential.

An interviewer for an influential international newspaper published in Paris recently asked for my viewpoints as to how acoustic and physiologic information serves the art of singing. A second interviewee in the same article took umbrage with what she called "scientific teaching," citing as example that she is strongly opposed to "raising her hard palate" as "science" advocated, but instead teaches how to spin "a golden thread of sound." (Indeed, it is well that she doesn't try to locally raise her hard palate, a physical impossibility, inasmuch as the hard palate is attached to the skull and could be elevated only were the skull to be lifted.) In all probability, she had confused the hard with the soft palate, which latter is bounded by fixated structures that also place limits on excessive palate elevation. Little wonder that she had little use for "science." However, her "golden thread" may have been more efficacious than the pseudo-scientific advice she had rejected!

Not long ago, a book reviewer for a prominent international opera journal wondered, "Why would Richard Miller think it important for a soprano to know where her diaphragm is?" The answer: because she will avoid much confusion about managing her breath if she does. Idiosyncratic assumptions about how the body works and pseudo-scientific speculation regarding physiology and acoustics are equal enemies of solid voice pedagogy.

All of this underscores the general dilemma that lies at the heart of teaching singing. If one cannot diagnose what is amiss, how can one make an effective prescription for improvement? What factors determine ideal vocalism? Is it "my fabulous ear" or is it the "fabulous ears" of others who may have different tonal goals? What gives me, as a teacher, the right to tell a student that one sound is better than another? Is it just a matter of personal preference, or are there determinables?

Much of this volume has been directed to the performer. At this point, I would like to suggest that there are specific principles that ought to guide anyone who teaches singing. When I moved from a full-time singing career to a performance/teaching role, I drew up a list of questions to which I have periodically returned. The answers to these interrelated questions make up what I came to call my "Ten Commandments of Voice Pedagogy." I respectfully share them with the reader.

1. Is the information I am about to deliver to the trusting person who stands before me determinable and verifiable?
2. Do I use precise, specific language or do I veil my pedagogy in the language of mystery and make-believe?
3. Am I willing to take singers at the level at which they find themselves, and assist them in moving forward?
4. Do I treat the student with complete respect, regardless of attainment level?
5. Do I understand the differences between voice-building and musical coaching? Am I adequately equipped to put both to use?
6. Do I make every minute of each lesson count? Do I give the student my full attention?

7. Is the lesson more about the student or about myself?
8. Do I point out what is good as well as what could be better? Do I build on what the student does well, and does the student leave the lesson with a sense of accomplishment?
9. Do I rely on generalized "filler," or does each lesson address the student's specific problems? Does it produce recognizable progress?
10. Do I possess sufficient information to diagnose problems and prescribe concrete solutions?

GLOSSARY

abdomen frontal body lying between the pelvis and the thorax.

abduction parting (as in opening the glottis).

acoustics (1) science of sound, including its production, transmission, and effects, (2) the sum of the qualities of an enclosure that partially determine the nature of the sound generated within it.

adduction coming together (as in the closure of the glottis).

aggiustamento system of vowel modification for the achievement of an equalized scale throughout the registers of the singing voice.

alveolar consonants voiced and unvoiced consonants articulated or produced with the tongue apex touching the upper front alveolar ridge.

anterolateral in front and to the side.

appoggio international breath-management technique in singing that induces coordination among the large, flat abdominal muscles of the antero-lateral wall and of the thoracic cage.

approximate to approach or produce vocal-fold contact or closure at the median position (see adduction).

arrotondamento the process of vowel rounding; a form of vowel modification.

articulators tongue, lips, teeth, hard and soft palates, which participate in determining the acoustic properties of the vocal tract.

arytenoid paired cartilage, to which the vocal folds attach, situated at the upper back part of the larynx; the arytenoids swivel outward as the glottis opens, then inward as the glottis closes.

atmospheric pressure exerted by the atmosphere in every direction, at approximately fifteen pounds per square inch at sea level.

attacco del suono vocal onset; the "attack."

axial position real or imaginary line maintained by the head, neck, and shoulders, regardless of postural location during singing.

Bauchaussenstütze "belly breathing"; distention of the lower abdominal wall; breath-management technique associated with a major segment of the German School.

bel canto "beautiful singing"; style of vocalism that unites tonal beauty and technical skill; frequently used to describe solo voice literature and the cultivated style of singing practiced before the mid-nineteenth century, as in the music of Bellini, Donizetti, and Rossini.

bilabial phonation formed with the aid of both lips, as in [p], [b], and [m].

breath management control of the inspiratory/expiratory components of the breath cycle, efficiently uniting myoelastic and aerodynamic aspects of phonation.

buccal cavity mouth cavity; oral cavity.

buccopharyngeal resonator resonance cavity formed by the mouth and the pharynx.

cabaletta second section of the opera *scena* form, written in florid or dramatic style, in contrast to the lyrical cantilena section that precedes it.

cartilage nonvascular connecting tissue, more flexible than bone (as in the cartilages of the larynx).

cartilaginous characterized or formed by cartilage.

cavatina graceful, flowing melody in "singing" style.

"chest voice" subjective term for sensations of sympathetic vibration experienced in the low range where the "heavy mechanism" is prominent: modal range.

chiaroscuro tone dark-light timbre of professional vocalism, achieved by a balance of the fundamental and its generated overtones (harmonic partials); proper relationship of the formants of the singing voice.

continuant speech or sung sound that may be prolonged within a single breath (as in a nasal continuant).

copertura (1) gradual modification of the vowel in a mounting scale, (2) the acoustic adjustments that result from altering the shapes of the resonator tract, (3) a component of aggiustamento in achieving *voce chiusa* as opposed to *voce aperta* timbre.

costal pertaining to a costa or rib, as in intercostal.

couverture (see copertura).

cover (covering) equates with copertura (see copertura) or may denote a suddenly darkened or somber voice timbre induced by excessive laryngeal depression.

cricoarytenoids muscles that rotate the arytenoid cartilages on the cricoid cartilage.

cricoid cartilage paired cartilage that articulates with the lower horn of the thyroid cartilage.

cricothyroids muscles attached to the front of the cricoid cartilage that can alter relationships of the thyroid and cricoid cartilages.

Deckung technique of laryngeal and acoustic alteration of timbre, especially in ascending vocal scale, accomplished by laryngeal depression and pharyngeal spreading; chiefly associated with an older part of the German/Nordic School.

diaphragm respiratory organ composed of muscle and sinew separating the respiratory and digestive systems; partition between the chest and the abdominal cavities.

dorsal of the back.

dynamic equilibrium cooperation among the muscles of the torso, the thorax, and the laryngeal musculature that avoids static positioning of any part of the respiratory/phonatory instrument; brought about by the appoggio breath management system.

electroglottography device for measuring changes in impedance (glottal resistance). (Two electrodes are placed on opposite sides of the thyroid cartilage of the larynx to register a waveform for visual display.)

epiglottis one of three single cartilages of the larynx; located between the root of the tongue and the entrance to the larynx.

esophagus tube that leads from the pharynx to the stomach; situated posteriorly to the trachea; the food track.

external oblique muscle whose fibers run mostly downward, forming layers of the lateral walls of the abdomen, fusing with the internal oblique to form the linea alba.

fach term used to distinguish one category of the singing voice from another.

falsetto (1) in historic voice pedagogy, a male timbre imitative of the female voice, (2) among voice therapists and researchers, any voiced sound that lies above the modal register.

fascia (fasciae) sheet or layer of connective tissue that covers, sheaths, supports, or binds together internal parts of structures of the body; as in the facial fascia.

fauces (isthmus of the fauces) passage located between the velum and the base of the tongue, leading from the mouth to the pharynx; space surrounded by the soft palate, the palatine arches, and the base of the tongue; the pillars of the fauces consist of two folds on either side of the faucial isthmus.

fioriture ornaments, florid embellishments, and cadences.

formant concentration of acoustic energy peaks originated by breath action on the resonance chambers, producing spectral regions of prominent energy distribution; spectral determinant of vowel differentiation, resonance balance, and timbre.

frequency number of vibrations per second; the greater the number, the higher the pitch.

fry (vocal fry) prolonged vocal-fold rattle, a "frying" sound produced by non-periodic vocal-fold vibration; a glottal scrape, rattle, or click; used as a research tool, it has no practical application to public performance.

gemischte Stimme mixed voice.

glottis alterable space between the vocal folds.

harmonic partial overtone or upper partial; vibration frequency that is a multiple of the vibration rate produced at the fundamental frequency.

"**head voice**" subjective term used to denote the upper range of the singing voice, produced by adjustments of the vocal folds and the vocal tract.

heavy mechanism pedagogic term describing variations in the internal contractions in the body of the vocal folds and tensions in the vocalis muscle.

hyoid bone U-shaped bone situated at the base of the tongue; from it the larynx is suspended.

hyperfunction excessive activity in any part of the physical mechanism.

hypofunction insufficient activity in any part of the physical mechanism.

Hz unit of measurement applied to the number of cycles per second (as in 440Hz); named for the physicist Heinrich Hertz.

imposto (impostazione della voce) "placement of the voice" (a subjective pedagogic term).

intercostals short external and internal muscles located between the ribs.

internal oblique abdominal muscle whose fibers mostly run upward, producing an abdominal-wall layer; it fuses with the external oblique to form the linea alba.

intrinsic on the inside; within (as the intrinsic muscles of the larynx).

laryngeal prominence externally visible portion of the larynx; "Adam's apple."

latissimus dorsi broad superficial muscle of the back.

levator muscle that raises or elevates (as in the levator anguli oris, levator scapula, levator veli palatini).

light mechanism term used in some pedagogies to describe dominant vocal ligament activity; frequently refers to "head voice."

linea alba median, tendinous division defining right and left sides of the abdominal musculature.

lingual of the tongue.

lutta vocale (*lutte vocale*) vocal contest; a description of abdominal muscle antagonism experienced during the appoggio.

mandible jaw.

manubrium uppermost portion of the sternum; its position is crucial to the maintenance of an axial posture and to proper breath management for singing.

marking (*markieren*) sparing the voice during rehearsal or illness through the reduction of dynamic levels; indicating certain pitches as opposed to singing them fully.

mask (masque) popular term for the zygomatic facial region.

maxilla (maxillae) region between the lips and the cheeks.

melisma rapidly moving notes on a single syllable; a run; a velocity passage.

myoelastic property of elasticity in muscles, as in the vocal folds.

myoelastic/aerodynamic theory of voice production vocal-fold vibration as the result of muscle tautness and breath pressure.

nuchal area of the nape of the neck.

obicularis oris muscle encircling the mouth.

occlusion closure (as in glottal occlusion).

onset (l'attacco del suono) commencement of phonation.

oscillation backward and forward motion; pitch fluctuation; may refer to pitch variant that is too wide and too slow; a "wobble."

overtone harmonic; multiple of a fundamental frequency.

palate roof of the mouth, composed of the hard palate and the posterior soft palate.

partial harmonic component of a complex voiced tone; overtone.

passaggio register pivotal point (as in primo passaggio, secondo passaggio).

pectoral pertaining to the chest.

phonation voicing; sound produced by the vibrating vocal folds.

phoneme speech or language sound identifiable regardless of spelling, as with [ɛ] in *get, tell, any, says.*

placement subjective term denoting sensations of sympathetic vibration.

platysma broad, thin muscle lying on either side of the neck under the mandible; a superficial facial muscle, sometimes known as the "grimacing muscle."

plosive speech sound formed by a complete stop closure, or by audible air released by an articulator or the glottis.

proprioception awareness of stimuli produced by one's own tension, relaxation, movement, or function, resulting in muscular, vibratory, or auditory sensation.

pyriform sinus space between the laryngeal collar and the alae of the thyroid cartilage; contributes to vocal-tract resonance.

rectus abdominis a long flat muscle located at both sides of the linea alba, extending the length of the abdomen; arises from the pubic crest and inserts into the cartilage of the fifth, sixth and seventh ribs; its upper three-fourths is enclosed in the rectus sheath formed by the aponeuroses of the external and internal oblique muscles ventrically, and the internal oblique and transversus abdominis muscles dorsally.

register consecutive tones of similar quality.

respiration breathing; exchange of internal and external gasses; the inhalation/exhalation cycle.

respiratory passage complex composed of the nostrils, the nasal cavities, the pharyngeal cavities, the oral cavity, the larynx, the trachea, the bronchi, and the lungs.

risorius narrow band of muscle fiber arising from the fascia over the masseter (chewing muscle), inserted into tissue at the corners of the mouth; a muscle of the cheek; sometimes termed "the smiling muscle."

scalenus (scaleni) deep muscle(s)—anterior, medius, posterior—on each side of the neck, extending from the transverse process of two or more cervical vertebrae to the first or second rib; accessory muscle of respiration.

serratus muscle arising from the ribs and vertebrae; popularly known as "the boxer's muscle."

sibilant speech phoneme characterized by a hissing sound, as in /s/ or /z/.

sinus cavity, recess, or depression, as the paranasal sinuses or the ventricular sinuses.

sinuses of Morgagni sinuses of the larynx; contributors to intralaryngeal resonance.

sostenuto sustained.

spectrography way of measuring and displaying the fundamental and overtone amplitudes generated by phonation; the first formant displays acoustic energy in the lowest regions of the spectrum; vowel definition is indicated largely by the shifting harmonics of the second formant at specific points in the spectrum; the singer's formant displays strong acoustic energy in the upper regions of the spectrum; balanced relationships among the fundamental and the formants produce the chiaroscuro tone of the cultivated singing voice.

sphincter a ring-like muscle around an orifice, capable of inducing closure, as with the laryngeal and anal sphincters.

sternocleidomastoid thick superficial muscle on each side of the neck, arising from the sternum and the clavicle and inserting into the mastoid bone; participates in the external-frame support of the larynx.

straight tone timbre devoid of vibrato, manifested in reduced spectral energy.

Strohbass (Schnarrbass) male low register, located below normal pitches of the speech-inflection range; induced by laryngeal depression.

subglottic below the glottis.

supraglottic above the glottis.

thorax region of the torso housing the organs of breathing; situated between the neck and the abdomen, supported by the ribs, the costal cartilages, and the sternum.

thyroid cartilage superior, largest single cartilage of the larynx; the most visible part of the laryngeal prominence.

trachea windpipe; main tubular system by which air passes to and from the lungs.

transverse abdominis deep abdominal muscle that works synergistically with other abdominal muscles in successful breath management.

trapezius large, flat, triangular muscle that covers the upper back; important postural muscle.

tremolo a pitch variant that is excessively rapid, with narrow pitch excursion; perceived as a markedly fast vibrato rate.

uvula fleshy pendant lobe located in the middle of the posterior part of the soft palate.

velum membranous partition; muscle portion of the soft palate that helps determine degrees of closure or opening of the velopharyngeal port.

ventricle cavity or pouch, as in the laryngeal ventricles.

vibrato desirable natural pitch variation, the result of neurological impulses during proper coordination of airflow and vocal-fold approximation; a laryngeal relaxant principle characteristic of cultivated singing.

vocal bands or **vocal folds** (true vocal cords) lower portion of the thyroarytenoid muscles.

vocalis muscle portion of the thyroarytenoid complex that includes the vocal folds; controls tensions in the body of the fold, and contributes in a major way to "chest voice" production.

vocal ligament portion of the vocal folds; active in "head voice" production.

vocal tract resonator tube of the voice; extends from the internal laryngeal lips to the external facial lips.

voce aperta "open" tone; lacking in proper chiaroscuro balance.

voce chiusa well-balanced resonance; avoidance of *voce aperta*.

voce completa complete resonance balance, regardless of range, dynamic, or velocity.

voce coperta equalized timbre through proper aggiustamento of the vowel in ascending scale; avoidance of shrillness or blatancy.

voce di petto (see "chest voice").

voce di testa (see "head voice").

voce finta "feigned" voice; disembodied timbre performed at piano dynamic, achieved through reduction of breath energy.

voce intermedia (see zona di passaggio).

voce mista "mixed" voice; subjective pedagogic term.

voce piena "full" voice.

wobble (see oscillation).

xiphoid process lowest (inferior) portion of the sternum.

zona di passaggio (passage zone) middle voice; area of the voice between the primo and the secondo passaggi.

zygomatic arch bone that extends along the front and side of the skull, formed by the union of the zygomatic process of the temporal bone with the zygomatic bone at the cheek area.

zygomatic bone facial bone, below the eyes.

zygomatic muscles slender bands of muscle on either side of the face, arising from the zygomatic bone and inserting into the orbicularis oris and the skin at the corners of the mouth; contributors to pleasant facial expression.

SELECT BIBLIOGRAPHY

Agostini, Emilio. "A Graphical Analysis of Thoraco-Abdominal Mechanics during the Breathing Cycle." *Journal of Applied Physiology* 15 (1961): 349–353.

———. "Diaphragm Activity and Thoraco-Abdominal Mechanics during Positive-pressure Breathing." *Journal of Applied Physiology* 17 (1961): 215–220.

———. "Dynamics." In *The Respiratory Muscles*, ed. E. J. Campbell, E. Agostini, and J. Newsom Davis, 2nd ed., 80–113. London: Lloyd-Luke (Medical Books), 1970.

———. "Kinematics." In *The Respiratory Muscles*, ed. E. J. Campbell, E Agostini, and J. Newsom Davis, 2nd ed., 23–47. London: Lloyd-Luke (Medical Books), 1970.

Agostini, Emilio, P. Mognoni, G. Torri, and F. Saracino. "Relation between Changes of Rib Cage Circumference and Lung Volume." *Journal of Applied Physiology* 20 (1965): 1179–1186.

———. "Static Features of the Passive Rib Cage and Abdomen-Diaphragm." *Journal of Applied Physiology* 20 (1965): 1187–1189.

Aiken, W. A. *The Voice: An Introduction to Practical Phonology.* London: Longmans Green, 1910; Minneapolis: University of Minnesota Press, reprint, 1951.

Amerman, J. D., R. G. Danilofff, and M. L. Moll. "Lip and Jaw Co-Articulation for the Phoneme /œ/." *Journal of the Acoustical Society of America* 13 (1970): 147–161.

Ansaldo, Lea, and Eldes Bassetti. *La voce dell'attore e la voce del cantante.* Genoa: Sabatelli Editore, 1977.

Appelman, D. Ralph. *The Science of Vocal Pedagogy* (1967). Bloomington: Indiana University Press, reprint, 1974.

Armin, Georg. *Die Technik der Breitspannung: Ein Beitrag über die horizontal-vertikalen Spannkrafte beim Aufbau der Stimme nach dem "Stauprinzip."* Berlin: Verlag der Gesellschaft für Stimmkultur, 1933.

Astraquillico, Corbelita, Irving Blatt, Leo Hoppel, and Robert Martinez. "Investigation of the Relationship between Abdominal Muscular Discipline and the Art of Singing: an Electromyographic Study." *American Academy of Ophthalmology and Otolaryngology* (1977): 498–519.

Austin, Stephen F. "Chi non lega, non canta: He Who Does Not Join His Notes, Cannot Sing." *Journal of Singing* 60.3 (2004): 301–303.

———. "Register Unification—Give Me a Break!" *Journal of Singing* 61.2 (2004): 199–203.

———. "Staccato." *Journal of Singing* 60.4 (2004): 405–407.

———. "The voce chiusa." *Journal of Singing* 61.4 (2005): 421–426.

———. "Treasure 'Chest'"—A Physiological and Pedagogical Review of the Low Mechanism." *Journal of Singing* 61.3 (2005): 241–252.

Bachner, Louis. *Dynamic Singing.* London: Dobson, 1940.

Bairstowe, Edward C., and Harry Plunkett Green. *Singing Learned from Speech.* London: Macmillan, 1945.

Baken, R. L., and S. A. Cavallo. "Prephonatory Chest Wall Posturing." *Folia Phoniatrica* 33 (1981): 193–203.

Baker, George. *The Common Sense of Singing.* London: Pergamon Press, 1963.

Balk, Wesley. *The Complete Singer-Actor.* Minneapolis: University of Minnesota Press, 1973.

Bartholomew, Wilmer T. *The Acoustics of Music.* New York: Prentice Hall, 1942.

Beard, Charles. "Recognition of Chest, Head, and Falsetto Isoparametric Tones." *The NATS Bulletin:* 37.1 (1980): 8–14.

Behnke, Emil. *The Mechanism of the Human Voice.* London: J. Curwen & Sons, 1880.

Bell, Donald. "Breathing for Singing." *Journal of Singing* 61 (2005): 374–377.

Bergofsky, E. H. "Relative Contribution of the Rib Cage and the Diaphragm to Ventilation in Man." *Journal of Applied Science* 19 (1964): 698–706.

Blanton, P. L., and N. L. Briggs. "Eighteen Hundred Years of Controversy: The Paranasal Sinuses." *American Journal of Anatomy* 124 (1969): 135–148.

Bouhuys, Arend, ed. *Sound Production in Man: Annals of the New York Academy of Sciences.* New York: New York Academy of Sciences, 1968.

Bouhuys, Arend, D. F. Proctor, J. Mead, and K. H. Stevens. "Kinetic Aspects of Singing." *Sound Production in Man: Annals of the New York Academy of Sciences.* New York: New York Academy of Sciences, 1968.

Bouhuys, Arend, D. F. Proctor, J. Mead, and K .H. Stevens. "Pressure-Flow Events during Singing." *Sound Production in Man: Annals of the New York Academy of Sciences.* New York: New York Academy of Sciences, 1968.

Brand, Myra J. "Agility or Sostenuto? (Where to Begin)" *Journal of Singing* 61.1 (2004): 51–54.

Brewer, David J., ed. *Research Potentials in Voice Physiology.* Syracuse: State University of New York Press, 1964.

Briess, Bertram. "Voice Diagnosis and Therapy." In *Research Potentials in Voice Physiology,* ed. David W. Brewer, 259–295. Syracuse: State University of New York, 1964.

Brodnitz, Friedrich. *Vocal Rehabilitation: A Manual Prepared for the Use of Graduates in Medicine, American Academy of Ophthalmology and Otolaryngology.* Rochester, Minn.: Mayo Clinic, 1971.

———. "Voice Problems of the Actor and Singer." *Journal of Speech and Hearing Disorders* 19 (1954): 322–326.

Brown, Oren. "Sensations." *Journal of Singing* 58.3 (2003): 224–232.

Brown, William Earl. *Vocal Wisdom: Maxims of Giovanni Battista Lamperti.* Boston: Crescendo Press, 1973.

Buescher, Randy. "Postoperative Posture Memory Rehabilitation Using Speech Level Singing Exercises and Balanced Onsets." *Journal of Singing* 58 (2003): 3, 223–228.

Bunch, Meribeth. "A Survey of the Research on Covered and Open Qualities." *The NATS Bulletin* 33.3 (1977): 11–18.

———. *Dynamics of the Singing Voice.* New York: Springer-Verlag, 1982.

Burgin, John Carroll. "Contributions to Vocal Pedagogy 1972–1975." *The NATS Bulletin* 34.3 (1978): 13–22.

———. *Teaching Singing.* Metuchen, N.J.: Scarecrow Press, 1973.

Campbell, E. J. Moran. *The Respiratory Muscles and the Mechanics of Breathing.* Chicago: Year Book (Medical) Publishers, 1958.

Christiansen, Lindsey. "Messa di voce and Dynamic Control." *Journal of Singing* 61.3 (2005): 269–270.

Cleveland, Tom. "Acoustic Properties of Voice Timbre Types and Their Influence on Voice Classification." *The Journal of the Acoustical Society of America* 61 (1977): 1622–1629.

Clippinger, D. A. *The Head Voice and Other Problems.* Philadelphia: Oliver Ditson, 1917.

Coffin, Bertrand. *Historical Vocal Pedagogy Classics.* Metuchen, N.J.: Scarecrow Press, 1989.

———. "The Relation of the Breath, Phonation and Resonance in Singing." *The NATS Bulletin* 31.P3 (1975): 37–44.

Cranmer, Arthur. *The Art of Singing.* London: Dennis Dobson, 1957.

Curtis, H. H. *Voice Building and Tone Placing.* New York: D. Appleton, 1909.

Daniloff, Raymond D. "Supraglottic Aspects of Singing." Transcripts of the 9th Symposium, ed. Van Lawrence, 38–44. New York: *The Voice Foundation,* 1979.

Davis, Peter. "Sound and Fury" (Sherrill Milnes). *Opera News* 68.2 (2004): 32–37.

———. *The American Singer.* New York: Doubleday, 1997.

Davis, Richard. *A Beginning Singer's Guide.* Lanham, Md.: Scarecrow Press, 1998.

Delle Sedie, Enrico. *Estetica del canto e dell'arte melodrammatica.* Leghorn: Author, 1885.

Denes, Peter B., and Elliott N. Pinson. *The Speech Chain: The Physics and Biology of Spoken Language.* Garden City, N.Y.: Bell Telephone Laboratories, 1923.

De Young, Richard. *The Singer's Art.* Chicago: DePaul University, 1958.

Douglas, Jan Eric. "Teaching Breathing." *Journal of Singing* 61.5 (2005): 487–489.

Duey, Philip. *Bel Canto in its Golden Age.* New York: King's Crown Press, 1950.

Edwin, Robert. "The Dumbing-Down of Classical Singing." *Journal of Singing* 58.3 (2002): 253–254.

Faaborg-Anderson, Knud, and Aatto A. Sonninen. "The Function of the Extrinsic Muscles at Different Pitch Levels." *Acta Otolaryngologica* 49 (1958): 47l.

Feld, Steven, A. Fox, Thomas Porcello, and David Samuels. "Vocal Anthropology: From the Music of Language to the Language of Song." *A Comparison of Linguistic Anthropology,* ed. Alessandro Duranti, 321–345. Oxford: Blackwell Publishing, 2003.

Fields, Victor. "Art Versus Science in Singing: A Basic Approach for the Teacher." *The NATS Bulletin* 29 (1972): 26–29.

———. "Review of the Literature on Vocal Registers," *The NATS Bulletin* 26 (1970): 3–39.

———. *Training the Singing Voice.* New York: King's Crown Press, 1923.

Fillebrown, Thomas. *Resonance in Singing and Speaking.* Bryn Mawr, Pa.: 1911

Fleming, Renée. *The Inner Voice: The Making of a Career.* New York: Viking. 2004.

Freeman, Edward, ed. *The Porpora Tradition.* Milwaukee, Wisc.: Pro Musica Press, 1968.

Frisell, Anthony. *The Baritone Voice.* Boston: Bruce Humphries, 1972. Boston: Crescendo Press, reprint, 1972.

Fritzell, Bjorn. "Electromyography in the Study of Velopharyngeal Function—a Review." *Folia Phoniatrica* 31 (1977): 93–102.

Froeschels, Emil. "Chewing Method as Therapy: A Discussion with Some Philosophical Conclusions." *Archives of Otolaryngology* 66 (1952): 629–633.

———. "Nose and Nasality." *Archives of Otolaryngology* 66 (1957): 629–633.

Fuchs, Viktor. *The Art of Singing and Voice Technique.* London: Calder and Boyars, 1963.

Garcia, Manuel. *Garcia's Complete School of Singing* (a compilation of the editions of 1847 and 1872). London: Cramer, Beale, and Chappell, n.d.

———. "Observations on the Human Voice." *Proceedings of the Royal Society of London* (1854–1855): 399–410.

Gould, Wilbur J. "The Effect of the Respiratory and Postural Mechanisms upon the Action of the Vocal Folds." *Folia Phoniatrica* 23 (1977): 211–222.

Green, Harry Plunkett. (1912). *Interpretation in Song.* Reprint London; Macmillan, 1956.

Gregg, Jean Westerman. "From Song to Speech: Resonation and Articulation—A New Concept." *Journal of Singing* 58.2 (2001): 167–169.

Hagerty, R. F., M. J. Hill, H. S. Petit, and J. J. Kane. "Posterior Wall Movement in Normals." *Journal of Speech and Hearing Research* 1 (1958): 203.

Hall, George. "Thomas Hampson's Desert Island Baritones," *Opera News* 68.2 (2003): 18–22.

Harris, K. S. "Behavior of the Tongue in the Production of Some Alveolar Consonants." *Journal of the Acoustical Society of America* 35 (1963): 784.

Hattori, S., K. Yamamoto, and O. Fujimura. "Nasalization of Vowels in Relation to Nasals." *Journal of the Acoustical Society of America* 30 (1958): 267–274.

Helmholz, Hermann L. F. *On the Sensations of Tone.* Trans. Alexander J. Ellis. London: Longmans Green, 1875, reprint 1939.

Henderson, W. J. *Early History of Song.* London: Longmans Green, 1921.

———. *The Art of Singing.* London: Dial Press, 1938.

Herbert-Caesari, E. *The Science and Sensations of Tone*, 2nd ed., rev., reprint, Boston: Crescendo Publishers, 1968.

Heriot, Angus. *The Castrati in Opera.* London: Secker & Warburg, 1956, reprint New York: Da Capo Press, 1969.

Hines, Jerome. *Great Singers on Great Singing.* New York: Doubleday, 1982.

Hisey, Philip D. "Scientific versus Empirical Methods of Teaching Voice." *The NATS Bulletin* 28.2 (1971): 4–15.

Hixon, Thomas J., and Cynthia Hoffman. "Chest Wall Shape in Singing." *Transcripts of the Seventh Symposium, Care of the Professional Voice*, ed. V. Lawrence, 9–10. New York: The Voice Foundation, 1979.

Hixon, Thomas J., Joseph Langhans, and Judith R. Smitheran. "Laryngeal Airway Resistance during Singing." *Transcripts of the Tenth Symposium, Care of the Professional Voice*, ed. V. Lawrence, 60–65. New York: The Voice Foundation, 1982.

Hixon, Thomas J., J. Mead, and M. Goldman. "Dynamics of the Chest Wall during Speech Production: Function of the Thorax, Rib Cage, Diaphragm and Abdomen." *Journal of Speech and Hearing Research* 5 (1976): 35–58.

Holmes, Leslie. "A Conversation with Jose van Dam, Part II." *Journal of Singing* 60.1 (2003): 95–97.

Hume, Paul. "Game Plan for Disaster: The Right Singer in the Wrong Role." *The Washington Post*, February 13 (1977): G-5.

Hunter, Eric J., and Ingo R. Titze. "Overlap of Hearing and Voicing Ranges in Singing." *Journal of Singing*, 61.4 (2005): 387–392.

Husler, Frederick. *Das vollkommene Instrument.* Stuttgart: Belsar-Verlag, 1970.

Husler, Frederick, and Yvonne Rodd-Marling. *Singing: The Physical Nature of the Vocal Organ.* London: Faber and Faber, 1960.

Husson, Raoul. *La voix chantée.* Paris: Gauthier-Villars, 1960.

Isley-Farmer, Christine. "Legs to Sing On: A Practical Guide for Singers and Voice Teachers." *Journal of Singing* 61: 3 (2005): 293–299.

Judd, Percy. *Vocal Technique.* London: Sylvan Press, 1951.

Kahane, Joel. "Growth of the Human Prepubertal and Pubertal Larynx." *Journal of Speech and Hearing Research*, 25 (1982): 446–455.

Kantner, Claude, and Robert West. *Phonetics.* New York: Harper & Brothers, 1960.

Kelsey, Franklin. *The Foundations of Singing.* London: Williams and Norgate, 1950.

Kemper, Josef. *Stimmpflege.* Mainz: B. Schotts Söhne.

Kiesgen, Paul. "To Listen or Not to Listen." *Journal of Singing* 58.2 (2002): 135–137.

———. "Well, Voice Pedagogy Is All Subjective Anyway, Isn't It?" *Journal of Singing* 62.1 (2005): 41–44.

Klein, Herman. *An Essay on Bel Canto.* London: Oxford University Press, 1923.

Kofler, Leo. *The Art of Breathing as the Basis of Tone Production.* 6th ed. New York: Edward S. Werner, 1889.

Lablache, Louis. *Lablache's Complete Method of Singing: Or a Rational Analysis of the Principles According to Which the Studies Should be Directed for Developing the Voice and Rendering It Flexible, and for Forming the Voice.* Boston: Oliver Ditson, n.d.

Laczkowska, M. "Concerning the Function of the Velum." *Folia Phoniatrica* 13 (1961): 107–111.

Ladefoged, Peter. *Elements of Acoustic Phonetics.* Chicago: University of Chicago Press, 1962.

Lamperti, Francesco. *The Art of Singing.* Trans. J. C. Griffith. New York: G. Schirmer, 1890.

Lamperti, Giovanni Battista. *The Techniques of Bel Canto.* New York: G. Schirmer, 1905.

———. *Vocal Wisdom: Maxims of Giovanni Battista Lamperti*, ed. William E. Brown, reprint Boston: Crescendo Press, 1973.

Landeau, Michel. "Voice Classification." Trans. Harold T. Luckstone. *The NATS Bulletin.* 20.1 (1963): 4–7, 31.

Large, John W. "Acoustic Study of Register Equalization in Singing." *Folia Phoniatrica* 25 (1972): 29–61.

———. "The Male Operatic Head Register Versus Falsetto." *Folia Phoniatrica* 24 (1973): 19–29.

———. Editor. *Vocal Registers in Singing.* The Hague: Mouton, 1973.

Large, John W., and Thomas Shipp. "The Effect of Certain Parameters on the Perception of Vocal Registers." *The NATS Bulletin* 26.1 (1969): 12–15.

Large, John W., Edward Baird, and Timothy Jenkens. "Studies of the Male High Voice Mechanisms: Preliminary Report and Definition of the Term 'Register.'" *Journal of Research in Singing* 4.1 (1981): 26.

Lawrence, Van. "Handy Household Hints: To Sing or Not to Sing." *The NATS Bulletin* 37.3 (1981): 23–25.

———. "Nodules and Other Things That Go Bump in the Night." *The NATS Bulletin* 38.2 (1981): 27, 30.

———. "Nose Drops." *The NATS Bulletin* 39.2 (1983): 24–25.

———. "Will Knowing How My Voice Works Make Me a Better Singer?" *The NATS Bulletin* 40.4 (1984): 24–25, 31.

Lehmann, Lilli. *How to Sing.* New York: Macmillan, 1903.

Lehmann, Lotte. *More Than Singing.* London: Boosey and Hawkes, 1946.

Lieberman, Philip, and E. S. Crelin. "On the Speech of Neanderthal Man." *Linguistic Inquiry* 2 (1971): 203–222.

Lieberman, Philip, and Sheila Blumstein. *Speech Physiology, Speech Perception, and Acoustic Phonetics.* New York: Cambridge University Press, 1998.

Lindblom, Bjørn E. F., and Johan Sundberg. "Acoustical Consequences of Lip, Tongue, Jaw and Larynx Movements." *Journal of the Acoustical Society of America* 50 (1972): 1166–1179.

Lohmann, Paul. *Stimmfehler—Stimmberatung.* Mainz: B. Schotte's Söhne, 1933.

Luchsinger, Richard, and Godfrey E. Arnold. *Voice—Speech—Language.* Trans. Godfrey Arnold and Evelyn Robe Finkbeiner. Belmont, Calif.: Wadsworth, 1965.

Mackinley, M. Sterling. *The Singing Voice and Its Training.* London: George Rutledge & Sons, 1910.

Mancini, Giovanni Battista. (1774). *Practical Reflections on the Art of Singing.* Trans. Pietro Buzzi. Boston: Oliver Ditson, 1910.

Manén, Lucie. *The Art of Singing.* London: Faber Music, 1974.

Marafioti, P. Mario. *Caruso's Method of Voice Production: The Scientific Culture of the Voice.* New York: Appleton, 1923.

Marchesi, Mathilde. (1903). Bel Canto. *A Theoretical and Practical Vocal Method.* Reprint New York: Dover, 1970.

Marchesi, Salvatore. *A Vademecum.* New York: G. Schirmer, 1902.

Mari, Nanda. *Canto e voce.* Milan: G. Ricordi, 1970.

Martiensen-Lohmann, Franziska. *Der Opernsänger.* Mainz: B. Schott's Söhne, 1943.

———. *Der wissende Sänger.* Zurich: Atlantis-Verlag, 1963.

Mason, R. M., and W. R. Zemlin. "The Phenomenon of Vocal Vibrato." The *NATS Bulletin* 22 (1966): 12–17; 18–23.

McClone, R. E., and W. S. Brown, Jr. "Identification of the 'Shift' between Registers." *Folia Phoniatrica* 18 (1969): 3013–322.

McIver, William, and Richard Miller. "A Brief Study of Nasality in Singing." *Journal of Singing* 4 (1996): 21–26.

McKinney, James. *The Diagnosis and Correction of Vocal Faults.* Nashville, Tenn.: Boardman Press, reprint San Diego: Singular Press, 1982.

Meano, Carlo. *La voce umana nella parola e nel canto.* Milan: Casa Editrice Ambrosiana, 1967.

Miller, Donald G., and Harm K. Schütte. "Toward a Definition of Male 'Head' Register, Passaggio, and 'Cover' in Western Operatic Singing." *Folia Phoniatrica Logopaedica* 46 (1994): 157–170.

Miller, Donald G., and James Doing. "Male Passaggio and the Upper Extension in the Light of Visual Feedback," *Journal of Singing* 4 (1998): 3–13.

Miller, Frank. *Vocal Art-Science and Its Application.* New York: G. Schirmer, 1917.

Miller, Richard. "Historical Overview of Vocal Pedagogy." *Vocal Health and Pedagogy,* ed. Robert T. Sataloff. San Diego: Singular Publishing, 1998.

———. *National Schools of Singing,* Metuchen, N.J.: Scarecrow Press, 1997.

———. *On the Art of Singing.* New York: Oxford University Press, 1997.

———. "The Odyssey of Orpheus: The Evolution of Solo Singing." *Voice Perspectives,* ed. Robert T. Sataloff. San Diego: Singular Publishing, 1998.

———. "The Problem of the Retroflex Tongue and of Pulling the Jaw Downward." *Journal of Singing* 58.3 (2002): 241–243.

———. *The Structure of Singing.* New York: Schirmer Books Macmillan, 1986.

———. "The Unique Teacher." *Journal of Singing* 59.4 (2003): 317.

Miller, Richard, and Harm K. Schütte. "The Effect of Tongue Position on Spectra in Singing." *The NATS Bulletin* 37.3 (1981): 26–27.

Mills, Wesley. *Voice Production in Singing and Speaking.* 2nd ed. Philadelphia: J. P. Lippincott, 1908.

Minifie, Fred D., Thomas J. Hixon, and Frederick Williams. *Normal Aspects of Speech, Hearing, and Language.* Englewood Cliffs, N.J.: Prentice Hall, 1973.

Moore, Dale. K. "To Listen or Not to Listen (to One's Own Voice)." *Journal of Singing* 59.3 (2003): 229–232.

Mori, Rachel Maragliano. *Coscienza della voce nella scuola italiana di canto.* Milan: Edizione Curci, 1970.

Nadoleczny. M. *Untersuchungen über den Kunstgesang.* Berlin: Verlag Julius Springer, 1923.

Nair, Garyth. "The Term Falsetto: Navigating Through the Semantic Minefield." *Journal of Singing* 60.1 (2003): 53–60.

———. *Voice–Tradition and Technology. A State-of-the-Art Studio.* San Diego: Singular Publishing, 2000.

Negus, Sir Victor E. *The Comparative Anatomy and Physiology of the Larynx.* London: William Heinemann Medical Books, 1949. New York, Hafner Publishing, reprint, 1962.

———. Falsetto. *The New Grove Dictionary of Music and Musicians,* ed. Eric Blum, 5th ed. New York: St. Martin's Press 3 (1966): 13–14.

Nix, John. "Vowel Modification Revisited." *Journal of Singing* 61.2 (2004): 173–176.

Paget, Sir Richard. *Human Speech.* New York, Harcourt, 1930.

Panofka, Heinrich. *Abécédaire vocale.* Paris, 1858.

———. *L'art de chanter.* Paris, 1854.

———. *Practical Singing Tutor.* London, 1852.

———. *Vademecum de chanteur* Paris, 1854.

———. *Voix et chanteurs.* Paris, c. 1870.

Patenaude-Yarnell, Joan "A Delicate Balance: Developing an Individual Approach to the New Student." *Journal of Singing* 58.3 (2002): 233–256.

———. "Sensations of Singing: A Look at Time-Honored Maxims, Descriptions and Images." *Journal of Singing* 60.2 (2003): 185–189.

———. "Teaching Breathing," *Journal of Singing* 61.5 (2005): 207–228.

———. "The Most Frequent Technical Problems Found in Young Singers." 60.5 (2004): 491–495.

Pettersen, Viggo, and Rolf H. Westgaard. "The Activity Patterns of Neck Muscles in Professional Classical Singing." *Journal of Voice* 19.2 (2005): 238–251.

Pleasants, Henry. *The Great Singers: From the Dawn of Opera to Our Own Time.* New York: Simon and Schuster, 1966.

Proctor, Donald F. The Physiologic Basis of Voice Training. In *Sound Production in Man,* ed. A. Bouhuys. New York: New York Academy of Sciences, 1965.

Punt, Norman. *The Singer's and Actor's Throat.* 3rd ed. London: Heinemann Medical Books, 1979.

Regier, Marvin P. *The Haute-Contre Voice: Tessitura and Timbre.* Doctoral Dissertation, University of Oregon, 1996.

Reid, Cornelius L. *Bel Canto: Principles and Practices.* New York: Coleman-Ross, 1950.

———. *Psyche and Soma.* New York: Joseph Patelson Music House, n.d.

Rose, Arnold. *The Singer and the Voice.* London: Faber and Faber, 1962.

Rushmore, Robert. "The Nose." *Journal of Singing* 57: 1 (2002): 22–26.

———. *The Singer's Voice.* New York: Dodd Mead, 1971.

Sable, Barbara Kinsey. *The Vocal Sound.* Englewood Cliffs, N.J.: Prentice Hall, 1982.

Sataloff, Robert T. (Editor.) The Physics of Sound. *Vocal Health and Pedagogy,* 2nd ed. San Diego: Singular Press, 1998.

Sataloff, Robert T., Deborah Caputo, and Steven Levy. "Performance Anxiety: What Singing Teachers Should Know." *Journal of Singing* 56.5 (2000): 33–40.

Scholl, Christopher. "Agility or Sostenuto? (Where to Begin)" *Journal of Singing* 60 (2004): 467–468.

Schütte, Harm K., and Richard Miller. "Breath Management in Repeated Vocal Onsets." *Folia Phoniatrica* 36 (1985): 235–233.

———. "Differences in Spectral Analysis of a Trained and an Untrained Singer." *The NATS Bulletin* 42.2 (1983): 22–26.

———. "Individual Parameters of the Singer's Formant." *Folia Phoniatrica* 36 (1985): 295–298.

———. "Resonance Balance in Register Categories of the Singing Voice: A Spectral Analysis Study." *Folia Phoniatrica* 36 (1984): 225–232.

Seashore, Carl. "The Vibrato." *Experimental Studies.* Ames: University of Iowa Press, 1932.

Seiler, Emma. *The Voice in Singing*. Philadelphia: J. B. Lippencott, 1875.

Shakespeare, William. *Plain Words on Singing*. Bryn Mawr, Pa.: Oliver Ditson, 1921.

———. *The Art of Singing*. Bryn Mawr, Pa.: Oliver Ditson, 1921.

Sheldon, W. H. *The Varieties of Human Physique*. New York: Harper & Brothers, 1940.

Shipp, Thomas. "Effects of Vocal Frequency and Effort on Vertical Laryngeal Position." *Journal of Research in Singing* 7.2 (1984): 1–5.

———. "Vertical Laryngeal Position in Singing." *Journal of Research in Singing* 1.1 (1977): 16–24.

Shipp, Thomas, Rolf Leanderson, and Stig Haglund. "Contribution of the Cricothyroid Muscle to Vocal Vibrato." *Transcripts of the Eleventh Symposium, Care of the Professional Voice*, 131–133. New York: Voice Foundation, 1976.

Sieber, Ferdinand. *The Art of Singing*. Trans. F. Seeger. New York: William A. Pond, 1872.

Siff, Ira. "Most Valuable Player" (Tribute to Robert Merrill). *Opera News* 69.2 (2004): 23.

Slater, David D. *Vocal Physiology and the Technique of Singing: A Complete Guide to Teachers, Students and Candidates for the A.R.C.M., A L.R.A.M., and All Similar Examinations*. London: J. H. Harway, n.d.

Smith, Ethel. "An Electromyographic Investigation of the Relationship between Abdominal Muscular Effort and the Rate of Vocal Vibrato." *The NATS Bulletin* 26 (1970): 4–17.

Smith, Michael. The Effect of Straight-Tone Feedback on the Vibrato." *The NATS Bulletin* 28.4 (1971): 28–32.

Sonninen, Aatto A. "The External Frame Function in the Control of Pitch in the Human Voice." *Sound Production in Man,* ed. A. Bouhuys. New York: New York Academy of Sciences, 1968.

———. "The Role of the External Laryngeal Muscles in Length-adjustment of the Vocal Folds in Singing." *Acta Oto-larygologica* (suppl. 130), 1956.

Stampa, Aribert A. *Sprache und Gesang*. Kassel: Bärenreiter Verlag, 1956.

Stanley, Douglas. *The Science of Voice*. New York: Carl Fischer, 1929.

———. *Your Voice—Applied Science of Vocal Art*. New York: Putnam Publishing, 1945.

Stark, James. *Bel Canto: A History of Vocal Pedagogy*. Toronto: University of Toronto Press, 1999.

Steane, J. B. *Singers and Critics*. London: Gerald Duckworth and Co. 1995.

Stetson, Raymond. H. *Bases of Phonology*. Oberlin, Ohio: Oberlin College Press, 1945.

Stevens, Kenneth J., and Minoru Hirano. *Vocal-Fold Physiology*. Tokyo: Tokyo University Press, 1981.

Stockhausen, Julius. *Method of Singing*. Trans. Sophie Lowe. London: Novello, 1884.

Sundberg, Johan. "Chest Wall Vibrations in Singers." *Journal of Speech and Hearing* 26.3 (1983): 329–340.

———. "Formant Frequencies of a Bass Singer." *Speech Transmission Laboratory Quarterly Progress and Status Report* 1 (1974): 1–16.

———. "The Acoustics of the Singing Voice." *Scientific American*. 236.3 (1977): 82–91.

———. *The Science of the Singing Voice*. Dekalb: Northern Illinois University Press, 1987.

———, ed. "The Voice as a Ground Resonator: Research Aspects on Singing." *The Royal Swedish Academy of Music* 6–14, 1981.

———. "Vocal Tract Resonance," *Vocal Health and Pedagogy*, ed. Robert T. Sataloff. San Diego: Singular Publishing, 1998.

Sundberg, Johan, and J. Gauffin. "Amplitude of the Voice Source Fundamental and the Intelligibility of Super Pitch Vowels." *Journal of Research in Singing* 7.1 (1983): 1–5.

Taff, Merle E. "An Acoustic Study of Vowel Modification and Register Transition in the Male Singing Voice." *The NATS Bulletin* 22.2 (1965): 2–5.

Taylor, Robert M. "Acoustics for the Singer." *Emporia State Research Studies* 6 (1958): 5–35.

Titze, Ingo R. "Acoustic Interpretation of Resonant Voice." *Journal of Voice* 15.4 (2001): 519–528.

———. "How Can the Vocal Mechanism Be Tuned for Maximum Acoustic Output Power?" *The NATS Bulletin* 37.5 (1981): 30–31.

———. "The Larynx and the Ear—How Well Do They Match?" *Journal of Singing* 57.5 (2001): 41–43.

———. "Nasality in Vowels." *NATS Journal*, 43.4 (1987): 34–35, 37.

———. *Principles of Voice Production*. Englewood Cliffs, N.J.; Prentice Hall, 1994.

———. "What Determines the Elastic Properties of the Vocal Folds and How Important Are They?" *The NATS Bulletin* 37 (1981): 5–26.

———. "What Makes a Voice Acoustically Strong?" *Journal of Singing* 61 (2004): 63–64.

Titze, I., and Sung Min Jin. "Is There Evidence of a Second Singer's Formant?" *Journal of Singing* 59.4 (2005): 329–331.

Titze, Ingo R., and B. H. Story. "Acoustic Interactions of the Voice Source with the Lower Vocal Tract." *Journal of the Acoustical Society of America* 101 (1997): 2234–2243.

Tosi, Pier Francesco. *Observations on the Florid Song* (1743). Trans. J. E. Galliard. London: J. Wilcox, n.d., reprint London: Stainer & Bell, 1987.

Vaccai, Nicola. *Metodo pratico di canto italiano*. Milan, 1832

———. *Solfeggi progressivi ed elementari sopra parole di Metastasio*. Milan, 1832.

Van Deinse, J. B., and Goslings, V. R. O. *The Technique of Singing: A Comparative Study*. The Hague: Government Publishing House, 1982.

Van den Berg, Janwillem. "Myoelastic–Aerodynamic Theory of Voice Production." *Journal of Speech Research* 1 (1968): 227–244.

———. "Register Problems." *Sound Production in Man*, ed. A. Bouhuys. New York Academy of Sciences, 1968.

———. "Some Physical Aspects of Voice Production." *Research Potentials in Voice Physiology*, ed. David Brewer. Syracuse: State University of New York Press, 1964.

Vasta, Stephen Francis. "Songs for Low Voice," *Opera News* 68 (2003): 24–29.

Vennard, William. *Singing: The Mechanism and the Technic,* rev. ed. New York: Carl Fischer, 1967.

Von Békésy, Georg. *Experiments in Hearing.* Trans. and ed. E. G. Weaver. New York: McGraw-Hill, 1960.

————. "The Structure of the Middle Ear and the Hearing of One's Own Voice." *Journal of the Acoustical Society of America* 20 (1949): 749–760.

Wade, O. L. "Movements of the Thoracic Cage and Diaphragm in Respiration." *Journal of Physiology.* 124 (1954):193–212.

Ware, Clifton. *Adventures in Singing.* New York: McGraw-Hill, 1997.

————. *Basics of Vocal Pedagogy.* Minneapolis: University of Minnesota Press, 1998.

Warenskjold, Dorothy. "Agility or Sostenuto? (Where to Begin)" *Journal of Singing,* 61.2 (2004): 163–165.

Warman, E. B. *The Voice: How to Train It and Care for It.* Boston: Lee and Shepard, 1889.

Watson, Peter J. and Thomas Hixon. "Respiratory Kinematics in Classical (Opera) Singers." *Journal of Speech and Hearing Research* 28 (1985): 104–122.

Weiss, Deso A. "The Pubertal Change of the Human Voice." *Folia Phoniatrica* 2 (1950): 126.

Weiss, Deso A., and Helen Beebe. *The Chewing Approach in Speech and Voice Therapy.* Basel: S. Karger, 1950.

Westerman, Kenneth N. *Emergent Voice.* Ann Arbor, Mich.: privately published, 1949.

White, Ernest G. *Science and Singing.* 1909. Boston: Crescendo Publishers, reprint, 1969.

————. *Sinus Tone Production.* 1938. Boston: Crescendo Publishers, reprint, 1969.

Whitlock, Weldon. *Bel Canto for Twentieth Century.* Champagne, Ill.: Pro Musica Press, 1975.

————. *Facets of the Singer's Art.* Champagne, Ill.: Pro Musica Press, 1967.

————. *Profiles in Vocal Pedagogy.* Ann Arbor, Mich.: Clifton Press, 1975.

Wilcox, John C. *The Living Voice.* New York: Carl Fischer, 1945.

Winckel, Fritz. *Music, Sound, and Sensation: A Modern Exposition.* Trans. Thomas Binkley. New York: Dover Publications, 1968.

Witherspoon, Herbert. *Singing.* New York: G. Schirmer, 1925.

Wolf, Artur. *Criticism of One-Sided Singing Methods: Problems of Voice Training and Their Solution.* Trans. Bert Jahr. New York: Irene Tauber, n.d.

Wormhoudt, Pearl Shinn. *Building the Voice as an Instrument.* Oskaloosa, Iowa: William Penn College, 1981.

————. *With a Song in My Psyche.* Web site: Xlibris, 2003.

Zemlin, W. R. *Speech and Hearing Science: Anatomy and Physiology,* 2nd ed. Englewood Cliffs, N.J.: Prentice Hall, 1981.

Zielinski, Shirley. "To Listen or Not to Listen." *Journal of Singing* 58 (2002): 133–135.

INDEX